CODING FOR KIDS PYTHON

CODING
FOR KIDS
PYTHON

LEARN TO CODE WITH
50 AWESOME GAMES AND ACTIVITIES

ADRIENNE B. TACKE

ILLUSTRATIONS BY AMIR ABOU ROUMIÉ

ROCKRIDGE
PRESS

Interior and Cover Designer: Merideth Harte
Photo Art Director: Sue Bischofberger
Editor: Susan Randol
Production Editor: Andrew Yackira
Illustrations: Amir Abou Roumié

ISBN: Print 978-1-64152-175-8 | eBook 978-1-64152-176-5
R1

To the technologists of tomorrow

CONTENTS

INTRODUCTION

***Coding for Kids: Python* is a unique and fun introduction** to the Python programming language. Written for someone with absolutely no experience with coding, this book uses silly analogies, helpful examples, and many activities and games to help anyone learn how to code in Python!

Let me share a little about myself, your excited author: I am currently a full-time software engineer who finds joy and fulfillment in helping new and potential coders of all kinds. I've spent many hours volunteering at local elementary and high schools, speaking to students about careers in software development, and teaching the basics of coding. It is so fun to see the spark in someone's eye when they see the power of code. I wrote this book to spark the imagination and wonder of many more people!

Code is at the core of almost everything we use and love. We can write code to make games, create music and art, bring robots to life, and power almost anything that is electronic. When you realize how much coding is a part of the world of the future, it becomes so important to learn how it works! This book will help you do just that.

Coding is literally translating human ideas and actions into a language that computers can understand. Python is one of the languages, but there are many others—for example: JavaScript, C#, Ruby, and C++. Each of these languages tells the computer how to do something, but each one does it a bit differently. I chose Python for this book because it is very close to our speaking language of English, which makes the coding concepts I will introduce a little easier to understand. :)

The best part about coding is that you just need a computer and this book! From the first chapter to the last, I'll guide you through the coding concepts you need to know, with step-by-step instructions and examples, plenty of helpful screenshots, and simple explanations of the new programming terms you'll learn (all of which are also available for you in the handy glossary at the back of the book!). By the time you've finished this book, you'll be creating some really cool programs and even simple games that you can play with friends! Hangman, anyone?

Coding is one skill that you'll only learn by doing. That's why I've structured each chapter to walk you through the code as you follow along. This makes the book truly interactive, as you'll learn about a concept, write some code, understand what it's doing, read and learn a bit more, maybe fix a bug or two, and see the results of your code in real time! And to really help you understand the different coding concepts in this book, I've also included activities at the end of each chapter to help you test your knowledge, combine multiple concepts, and write more code. After all, practice makes perfect—especially with coding! Finally, if some of the activities are too easy for you, or if you just want to keep coding, I've included even more difficult challenges after each chapter to really stretch your brain and give you more chances to show off your creativity!

This book will help you start an incredible adventure into the world of programming. By the end of it, you'll be ready for the world of the future! What are you waiting for?

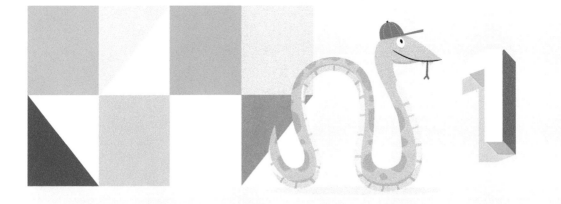

WELCOME TO PYTHON!

Hey there! Since you're reading this book, you must be a pretty curious and cool person. Why? Because you want to learn how to code! And who wouldn't? Coding is an awesome skill that can help you build all kinds of things and solve a lot of problems. When you code, you take human ideas and then translate them into a language that a machine can understand.

Coding is built around the concept of input and output. We give the computer some *input*, which is any information or data provided by us humans, and expect some *output*, which can be words, pictures, an action, or some other result, after the computer has processed the input we gave it. Sounds interesting, doesn't it?

How many things can you think of that follow this input/output, or *I/O*, concept? For example, when we press buttons on a controller or swipe our fingers left and right on a mobile game, that's input. And when our character jumps, ducks, moves left, or moves right, that's output. How about baking? All of the ingredients we need to make cookies can be considered input. After following the instructions and using the ingredients, we get our output, which are the baked cookies!

Using examples like these, as well as silly scenarios and conversations with a computer, we'll explore how to code in Python, and you'll understand what we're doing in no time! The coolest thing about coding is that you can do it from almost anywhere. All you need is a laptop or computer (Windows PC or Mac is fine), and I'll help you with the rest.

Are you ready to learn how to speak to a computer? Hooray! Let's go!

WHY PYTHON?

Just like humans can understand many different languages, a computer can understand the ideas and concepts that we input to it through several different programming languages. In this book, we'll focus on the Python programming language because Python is easy to understand, can be used in many different ways, and is quick to learn. Also, it is a popular language that runs on almost every machine and is used at many big, important organizations like Google, Instagram, NASA, and Spotify.

INSTALLING PYTHON

I know we want to dive right into coding, but we can't do that until we have the right tools. I'll walk you through the step-by-step process of installing Python. Let's get started!

ON A PC

If you are on a Windows machine, you probably don't have Python installed already. This is because Windows operating systems don't usually come with the Python language. That's okay, though! We can get it ourselves. :)

1. On your computer, open an Internet browser like Google Chrome or Mozilla Firefox.

2. In the address bar, type "https://www.python.org/downloads/" to go to the official Python website's Downloads section.

3. Through the magic of coding, the website will probably know what type of computer you are using, and the **DOWNLOAD** button will show you the correct version of Python to install! In our case, we want the latest version, which was Python 3.7.0 when I wrote the book. Don't worry if it tells you to download a newer version. Go ahead and click the **DOWNLOAD** button.

4. A download will start and will probably go to the bottom of your window like in the picture.

WELCOME TO PYTHON!

5. Once your download is complete, click on it to begin the installation. When you do, a window should pop up.

6. Go ahead and click the **RUN** button. Then, you'll see this window (yours may say 32-bit if that's right for your machine):

7. Make sure to check the **ADD PYTHON 3.7 TO PATH** checkbox.

☑ Add Python 3.7 to PATH

8. Click **INSTALL NOW**. Python should begin installing. You should see a window like this one:

9. Wait for the install to finish and the green bar to be full. Once it is done, the final screen should appear, saying that your installation was successful.

10. Whoo-hoo! You're done! Click the **CLOSE** button and you're ready to go. You've installed Python on Windows!

ON A MAC

1. On your computer, open an Internet browser like Google Chrome or Mozilla Firefox.

2. In the address bar, type "https://www.python.org/downloads/" to go to the official Python website's Downloads section.

3. Through the magic of coding, the website will probably know what type of computer you are using, and the **DOWNLOAD** button will show you the correct version of Python to install! In our case, we want the latest version, which was Python 3.7.0 when I wrote the book. Don't worry if it tells you to download a newer version. You can also find the installer for your specific machine in the Files section.

4. After clicking on the version, a download should start. Wait for it to finish before starting the installer.

5. When you start the installer, you should see a window like this one:

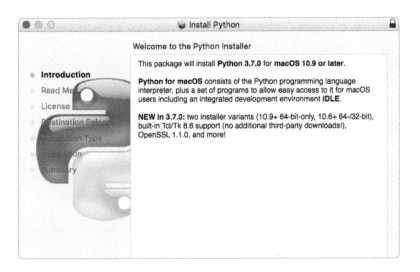

6. Click the **CONTINUE** button. You'll then be presented with some important information that you can choose to read or not.

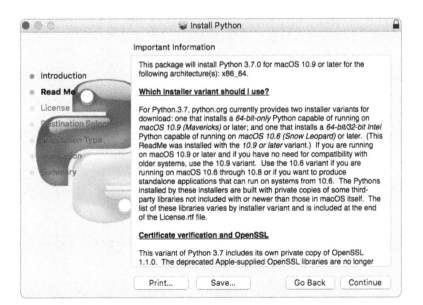

7. Click the **CONTINUE** button. Next you will see the license information.

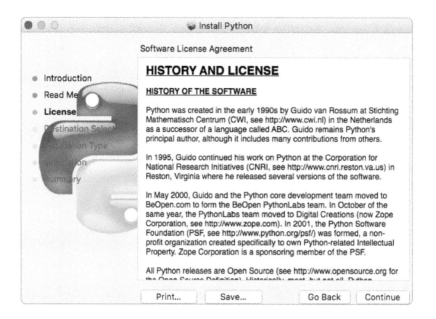

8. Keep going! Click the **CONTINUE** button. You'll be asked to agree to the terms of the software license agreement.

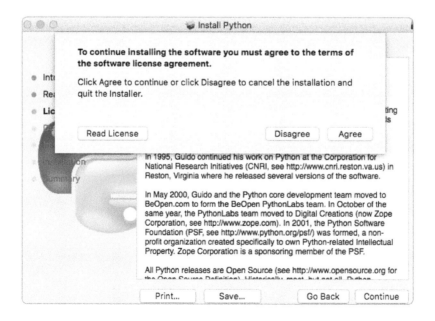

CODING FOR KIDS : PYTHON

9. Click the **AGREE** button. You'll reach this final window:

Install Python

Standard Install on "Macintosh HD"

- Introduction
- Read Me
- License
- Destination Select
- **Installation Type**
- Installation
- Summary

This will take 106.3 MB of space on your computer.

Click Install to perform a standard installation of this software on the disk "Macintosh HD".

Change Install Location...

Customize   Go Back   Install

10. Click the **INSTALL** button. If you need to, enter your personal user name and password for your account on your computer. Mac OS sometimes asks for this to make sure you want to install something. If you don't see this pop-up window, you can skip to the next step.

Installer is trying to install new software.

Enter your password to allow this.

User Name: Your Name

Password: ••••••••

Cancel   Install Software

11. Installation should begin.

12. Wait for the installation to finish. Once it is done, you should see this:

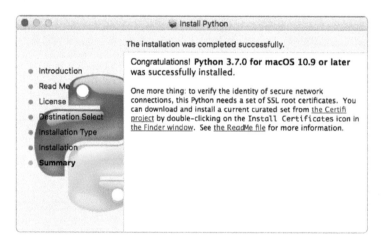

13. Congratulate yourself! You've just installed Python on your Mac!

>>> **YOU MAY HAVE NOTICED WE ASKED YOU TO TYPE** "https://www.python.org/downloads/".
But is that *https://* really necessary, or could we just start with *www*? The answer is this:
Python is good about redirecting you to the right site, but adding *https://* before typing
web addresses is a good practice to get into, so you can be sure your computer is going
to a secure site!

CODING FOR KIDS : PYTHON

USING IDLE

When you download and install Python, it will also install an application called IDLE. *IDLE* is short for Integrated Development and Learning Environment (that's a mouthful!), and it is an integrated development environment, or *IDE*, that helps us with writing Python programs. Think of it as an electronic notepad with some additional tools to help us write, debug, and run our Python code. To work in Python, you will need to open IDLE—opening Python files directly won't work!

Let's take a look!

ON A PC

1. Click the Windows Start menu.

2. Start typing "idle", then select the search result IDLE (Python 3.7 64-bit). Note: Yours might say IDLE (Python 3.7 32-bit) if that's the kind of machine you have.

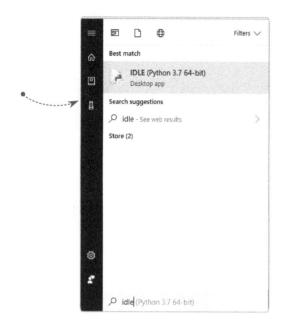

3. A window should pop up that looks like this:

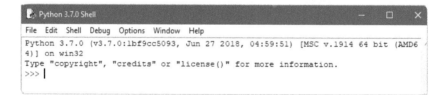

4. Ta-da! Awesome! You opened IDLE on Windows and are now ready to start writing some code in Python! :)

ON A MAC

1. Navigate to **GO** > **APPLICATIONS**.

2. Find the Python 3.7 folder and open it.

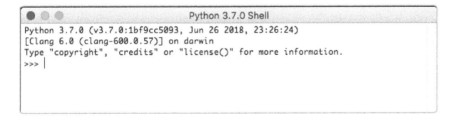

3. Double-click on the IDLE icon.

4. A window should pop up that looks like this:

```
Python 3.7.0 Shell
Python 3.7.0 (v3.7.0:1bf9cc5093, Jun 26 2018, 23:26:24)
[Clang 6.0 (clang-600.0.57)] on darwin
Type "copyright", "credits" or "license()" for more information.
>>>
```

5. Whoo-hoo! Congratulations! You opened IDLE on a Mac and are now ready to start writing some code in Python! :)

SAY HI TO PYTHON!

Now that you've installed Python and IDLE on your computer, let's say hi! Open up IDLE on your computer (if it's not already open). Whenever you open up the IDLE program on your computer, you will always be brought to the *shell* first. The shell is the interactive window that allows you to write Python code within it and then see the results of your code right away. You'll know when you're in the shell because it will say Python 3.7.0 Shell in the title bar of the window.

In your shell, go ahead and type the following code:

```
print("Hi Python!")
```

Now, hit the **ENTER** key. Do you see something like this?

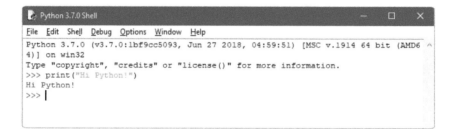

Great job! You've written your first line of Python code! Give yourself a pat on the back, or high-five the person closest to you. You're about to learn some awesome things.

SAVING YOUR WORK

When we get into the later chapters, our programs will probably be a little longer than the ones we write in the beginning. Wouldn't it be useful if we could save our progress so we don't have to re-type all the code we write? Of course it would! This is where saving your work comes in handy.

Even though it's a short program, let's save our Python greeting to its own file so you can see how easy it is to save your work.

First, let's create a new file:

1. On the **MENU** bar in your shell, click the **FILE** tab to open its context menu, which is a list of actions that you can perform.

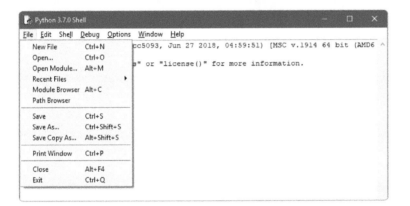

2. Click **NEW FILE**.

3. A new window should pop up, like this:

4. Type in your greeting, using Python code: **print("Hi Python!")**

We have to put our greeting into this piece of Python code so that the computer knows to "write" this message for us onto the screen. (You'll learn more about this later.)

Great! Now you have your code in a file that we can save. This is important, because the first code we wrote was in the shell, which means it won't be saved once you close the window. Writing code directly in the shell is just a quicker way to run Python code and see the results right away. Always create a new file and save it to keep track of your work and save your progress!

Now that we have created a file with our greeting code, let's save it.

You can save your program in IDLE by following these next steps.

5. On the **MENU** bar of your shell, click the **FILE** tab to open its context menu.

CODING FOR KIDS : PYTHON

6. Click **SAVE**.

Untitled

File	Edit	Format	Run	Options	Window	Help

New File   Ctrl+N
Open...   Ctrl+O
Open Module...   Alt+M
Recent Files   ▶
Module Browser   Alt+C
Path Browser

Save   Ctrl+S
Save As...   Ctrl+Shift+S
Save Copy As...   Alt+Shift+S

Print Window   Ctrl+P

7. The next window will ask you to name your file. Go ahead and give it a name. I'll call mine "greeting."

WELCOME TO PYTHON!

8. Make sure to save your Python program in a place that you won't forget! If you don't choose another place, new files are usually saved in the same folder as the Python download, so go ahead and change the "Save In" place to a better spot. I created a folder called **COOL PYTHON** in my **DOCUMENTS** directory, so that's where I'll save my programs.

9. Click **SAVE**. That's it!

⌗ HELPFUL HACKS: KEYBOARD SHORTCUTS

Saving files and our code is a big part of programming. We programmers do it so much that there are shortcuts created just for saving, among other things. Here's a list of very helpful keyboard shortcuts to use while coding.

CTRL **key + S key:** This is the standard save shortcut. You can press these two keys together to save your progress while coding or to save a new file!

CTRL **key + N key:** This shortcut will create a new file for you.

CTRL **key + C key:** This shortcut copies any text you have selected. Here's how: Use your mouse to highlight some text or code. To highlight text, place your cursor before the start of the text you want to copy, click and hold the main mouse button, drag your mouse to the end of the text you want to copy, and then release the mouse button. After your text is highlighted, use this shortcut to copy the highlighted text!

CTRL **key + V key:** After copying some text, use this shortcut to paste it. This places the text you have highlighted and copied wherever you choose.

CTRL **key + Z key:** The most awesome command, this shortcut performs an undo action. If you ever need to go back a step, or bring back some code you have accidentally deleted, this shortcut can save the day! Use this shortcut once, by pressing the CTRL key and Z key together, and watch your last change undo itself. You can keep pressing this shortcut multiple times to keep going back further and reversing more actions you have just performed. Remember though, this can't undo everything—it can only reverse actions up to the point that the computer has stored in its memory.

RUNNING A PROGRAM

This is the best part—seeing your code in action! After you write some code, save it, and are ready to see it run, follow these steps to run your code (skip to step 4 if you already have your program open in its own window).

1. On the **MENU** bar in your shell, click the **FILE** tab to open the context menu.

```
Python 3.7.0 Shell                                    —    □    ×

File  Edit  Shell  Debug  Options  Window  Help
   New File          Ctrl+N        cc5093, Jun 27 2018, 04:59:51) [MSC v.1914 64 bit (AMD6  ^
   Open...           Ctrl+O
   Open Module...    Alt+M         s" or "license()" for more information.
   Recent Files               ▶
   Module Browser    Alt+C
   Path Browser

   Save              Ctrl+S
   Save As...        Ctrl+Shift+S
   Save Copy As...   Alt+Shift+S

   Print Window      Ctrl+P

   Close             Alt+F4
   Exit              Ctrl+Q
```

2. Click **OPEN**.

```
Python 3.7.0 Shell                                    —    □    ×

File  Edit  Shell  Debug  Options  Window  Help
   New File          Ctrl+N        cc5093, Jun 27 2018, 04:59:51) [MSC v.1914 64 bit (AMD6  ^
   Open...           Ctrl+O
   Open Module...    Alt+M         s" or "license()" for more information.
   Recent Files               ▶
   Module Browser    Alt+C
   Path Browser

   Save              Ctrl+S
   Save As...        Ctrl+Shift+S
   Save Copy As...   Alt+Shift+S

   Print Window      Ctrl+P

   Close             Alt+F4
   Exit              Ctrl+Q
```

3. A window will pop up asking you to pick the file you want to open. Go ahead and find your greeting program and select it. Click **OPEN**.

4. Your program should open in its own window.

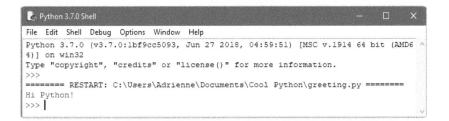

5. Press the F5 key. That's it! Your code should now *execute*, meaning the computer will carry out the task you asked it to do in code. You told it to print something, and it did! You should see your greeting in the shell.

>>> **TROUBLESHOOTING TIP:** Is the F5 key not working for you? Some computers require you to press the Fn button along with the F5 button. Go ahead, try that instead!

WELCOME TO PYTHON!

⌗ HELPFUL HACKS: RECENT FILES

Once you start writing more code, you'll find that you will have many Python files and programs in your folders. A cool thing that the IDLE program does is keep track of the most recent files you have worked with and make them easily available for you. To get to a file you have recently worked with, simply click the **FILE** tab on the **MENU** bar and hover your mouse over **RECENT FILES**.

You'll see the list of files appear that you have recently worked with. Clicking on one will open that file for you. Sometimes this is an easier way to get to a file you need, rather than hunting through your computer to find it!

PRINT("HELLO!")

One of the most used lines of code in Python is the **print()** function. We use it everywhere. Of course, you've already used it in the first chapter!

```
print("Hi Python!")
```

At its core, the **print()** function is used when we want to output a string. A *string* is a collection of characters, or what we know as text. Strings are a *type*—just like it sounds, a type is a way for the computer to understand what kind of input we are giving it. There are other types, like integers, Booleans, and lists—but don't worry about them yet! We'll learn about them later.

The **print()** function takes a few *parameters*, which are pieces of information (input) you give a function to do something with. For now, we'll only use one parameter, which is the part you put inside the double quotes. The **print()** function will take this piece and print it out to the console window.

Seeing information in the console window is very useful. If we write some code to show a greeting, we can use the **print()** function to see the greeting our code produces. Likewise, if we perform some basic math, the **print()** function can show us the resulting answer.

While coding, it is also very helpful to use the **print()** function for *debugging*, which is the quest we undergo to find issues or mistakes in our code that cause it to not work the way we want it to. These issues or mistakes in our code are called *bugs*. When we are in the middle of debugging, we can print out parts of our code to double-check that it is doing what we expect it to do. This process will come in handy later on as we deal with variables and decision-making blocks of code.

⌗ HELPFUL HACKS: COMMENTS AND DEBUGGING

A good habit to get into is to remove any **print()** functions you write that are not needed for your main program. You can remove them by deleting them completely or by using comments.

Comments are pieces of code that do not get translated by the computer. You use them as helpful messages you leave for yourself within your code, or as parts of code you want the computer to ignore. You can create a comment by putting a hash character (#) before the line you'd like the computer to ignore. This is also called commenting out a line. As you'll see, comments also become a noticeable red color to show you they are comments.

```python
# print("I should not be printed!")
```

So, if there's part of your code that you think is causing you problems, you don't have to delete it. You can test it by commenting it out:

```python
print("Hello")
# print("You are a silly shoe!")
```

In the code above, it would print the first line ("Hello"), but not the second ("You are a silly shoe!")—because the hash character signals to the computer, "Don't print this line!" How cool is that?

There are also times where you just need comments to help you remember or understand what your code is doing:

```python
# This code prints out text to the shell
print("Hello there!")
```

These types of comments will become very useful when you start writing longer programs!

TRICKY PRINTING

For the most part, you can use the **print()** function to write whatever you want to the console window. However, there are a few situations and special characters that the **print()** function doesn't play nice with—kind of like electronic troublemakers. Let's see "what," not "who" they are.

QUOTES AND APOSTROPHES

Let's say we wanted to print the following sentence: "I'm so happy to be learning how to code in Python!" Use the code below to print out the sentence:

```
print('I'm so happy to be learning how to code in Python!')
```

What happens? Are you able to see that sentence in your console window? If not, that's okay. In fact, that's supposed to happen. You probably just got your first syntax error, too! Congratulations, sort of.

Here's what's happening: When you use the **print()** function, you tell the computer, "Hey, I need you to write something out to the console window for me." The computer says, "Sure! Let me see exactly what you want me to write." The computer checks the **print()** function you wrote, and looks for a **starting quote** and an **ending quote**. To the computer, these quotes act as "flags" for the beginning and end of the information you wrote. So, once it finds the first and second quote in your string, it thinks it's done. It doesn't expect any other characters after the second quote it finds. When this happens, it sends a message back to you in the form of a *syntax error* (shown in the shell with the text **SyntaxError**).

Take another look at the sentence. Can you see where the problem is?

It is right at the beginning of our sentence! The first quote the computer finds is our normal starting quote. The next one, however, is a single quote (') or an apostrophe in the word "I'm." At this point, the computer says, "Hmm, well, this is the second quote in the string, so this should be the end. I don't understand all of this extra stuff after it, though. Better tell Human I don't get what he or she is trying to say." That's when you get the following syntax error.

```
Python 3.7.0 Shell                                          —  □  ×
File  Edit  Shell  Debug  Options  Window  Help
Python 3.7.0 (v3.7.0:1bf9cc5093, Jun 27 2018, 04:59:51) [MSC v.1914 64 bit (AMD6
4)] on win32
Type "copyright", "credits" or "license()" for more information.
>>> print('I'm so happy to be learning how to code in Python!')
SyntaxError: invalid character in identifier
>>>
```

But wait! You did provide the matching quote at the end of your sentence! You may be asking yourself, "Why didn't it find the right matching quote?" When the computer looks at the **print()** function, it only knows to look for the very first and second quote in the input you provide. Once it finds that second quote, everything else that comes after it is ignored.

So how do we fix this? We still want to write the full sentence, but we know that the computer will mistakenly think our ending flag is the apostrophe in the word "I'm." One solution is to use double quotes. For example:

```python
print("I'm so happy to be learning how to code in Python!")
```

This works because the computer sees that the first quote is a double quote. When it continues searching the string, it will only look for the second matching quote, which also needs to be a double quote. Note: In Python, you can use either *single quotes* or double quotes in coding, but try to stick with one or the other. This double quote is usually the best way to go when using strings!

Another solution to this problem is to use escape characters.

Escape Characters

In code, there are special characters called *escape characters* that allow us to give the computer a heads-up when we're going to pass some tricky information to it. For Python, this character is the backslash (\) character. There are two slash characters on your keyboard: the forward slash (/) and the backward slash (\), also called the backslash. You can keep them straight by checking which way the top of the slash "leans." The forward slash is the one that shares a key with the question mark, and the backslash is under the BACKSPACE key (delete key on a Mac).

To use it, we simply type a backslash before the tricky character. Using an escape character helps us "escape" the problem!

Let's fix our sentence from the previous section:

```python
print('I\'m so happy to be learning how to code in Python!')
```

Now try printing the sentence with our revised code. Did it work? Yay!

CODING FOR KIDS : PYTHON

This time, when the computer looks for the matching pair of quotes, it knows to skip the apostrophe in the word "I'm" because we told it to. It sees the escape character and says, "Oh, that's nice. Human was cool enough to let me know that this is definitely not the second quote. I'll keep looking!"

Escape characters are also really handy if you need to print more than one trouble-making character, like a single quote/apostrophe (') or double quote ("), and especially if they are all on one line!

For example, try printing this to your console window:

```
print("\"Kumusta\" is \"Hello\" in Tagalog!")
```

Do you see how the computer prints the words "Kumusta" and "Hello" with double quotes? Great! That's what we wanted. The quotes are printed to help show how the two words are closely related to each other. They are the same word in two different languages. Human languages, that is.

MULTIPLE LINES

Another troublemaker that the **print()** function has a hard time with is multiple lines. How can we print the following sentence, exactly as it appears?

Here is
a sentence
on many
different lines.

Well, we have a special escape character that the computer understands as a new line. In programming, we sometimes call a new line a *line break* or *line feed*. It's a backslash (\) and a lowercase letter "n" put together. It looks like this: **\n**. Using what you know about escape characters, try printing that sentence.

Did you write something like this?

```
print("Here is \na sentence \non many \ndifferent lines.")
```

Great! It looks a little funny when you type it, but as you can see when you print it out, it's correct. Remember, everything that is between your starting and ending quotes will be printed exactly as it is understood by the computer. This even includes line spaces!

Here's what's happening: Just as the \ escape character told the computer to ignore the apostrophe in our first example, the \n escape character tells it, "Hey, can you start writing everything after this \n flag on a new line?" And like a good friend, the computer will do just that every time you use the \n escape character.

VARIABLES

Now is a great time to talk about variables. Variables are another important part of coding because we use them all the time! It will also be good to get comfortable with them before we move onto the next sections.

A *variable* is just a fancy name for a tag, or a way to keep track of information. It's just like many tags we see in life:

- Some people wear name tags so we know who they are.

- Nutrition labels on food are tags. They tell us all kinds of information, like how many calories the food has, the grams of sugar it contains, or the list of ingredients used.

- Tags on clothing provide tons of information, including the size, designer, price, and sometimes even the identity of the person who inspected it.

It's really interesting to see coding concepts like this in real life. What's even cooler is that you probably didn't know that you would already be familiar with variables. Let's put that knowledge to good use in coding!

When we code, we use variables to hold pieces of information for us. And just like clothing tags and food labels, coding variables can hold many kinds of information, such as strings, numbers, lists, and more.

So how do we create one? Let's make a variable to keep track of the name of this book's author (hey, that's me!). We would create a variable like this:

```
author = "Adrienne"
```

That's all there is to it! The variable **author** is now a tag for the string "Adrienne."

Here's what's happening: When we create the variable, we give it a name: **author**. This helps us remember what the information is about. Next, we type an equal sign (=). This tells the computer that we are giving the **author** variable some information it should keep. This is called *assignment*, or assigning a variable, in programming. Finally, we type out the information our variable is supposed to keep track of. In this example, it's the name of the author, "Adrienne."

Now let's get *your* name involved! We'll create another variable called **reader**. Go ahead and assign your name to this variable. For this example, we'll use the name Casey. Then, on the next line, use the **print()** function to write your variable to the console. Your final code should look something like this:

```
reader = "Casey"
print(reader)
```

Now press **ENTER**. What happened? Do you see your name in the console window? Cool!

Now, here's the cooler part about variables: Let's say you share this book with your friend Alex. Obviously, our **reader** variable would now be incorrect—it should be your friend's name! Go ahead and change the **reader** variable so it is assigned to your friend's name, but change nothing else. With the change, your code should look like this:

```
reader = "Alex"
print(reader)
```

Now press **ENTER**. Did your friend's name print out this time? It did! So cool! We can thank the computer for this awesome superpower. How exactly does the computer do this, though?

When a computer sees a variable, it says, "Ooh, Human wants me to remember this piece of data. I better make some room in my *register* and store this data. I should also mark where I am storing this data so I can quickly get it if Human needs it again."

So organized, huh? And convenient. Computers are great! The register is basically a place within the computer's central processing unit that holds information. You can think of it as a big, grid-like bookshelf with many different cubbies to place things in. This grid system is a way that the computer marks the location of any data it stores so it can quickly remember where to get it if we need it again.

PRINT("HELLO!")

THE HISTORY OF THE LINE FEED

We know that the line feed escape character is used whenever we want to start printing a new line in our shell. But do you know where the term "line feed" comes from?

In the past, before there were computers, people used machines called typewriters. These were used to write papers and books like this one!

You may have seen one before, as they are hard to miss. This machine requires you to place paper in it in a very specific way, press really hard on the keys to print a letter onto the paper, and move different parts of the typewriter around. In order to move to the next line on your paper, some typewriters require you to turn the wheel that holds the paper so you can "feed" the machine another blank line of paper for you to type on. And that's where the term "line feed" comes from!

The variables we just used held strings (text), but like we mentioned earlier, variables can also hold other data types. If we wanted to create a variable to hold our favorite number, how would we do it?

```
favorite_number = 3
```

We create this in a similar way:

- We give our variable a name: **favorite_number**
- Then we assign it to a piece of information. In this case, it's the number **3**.

Did you notice that we didn't use quotes around our number this time? Can you guess why?

Just as we use string types to tell the computer we are giving it text input, we use integer types to tell the computer that we are using whole numbers. In Python, whole numbers are known as *integers*.

Whenever we deal with integers, we just type them out as a plain number, like we are used to seeing. You don't use quotes around them, as that will confuse the computer into thinking you are using a string! To see what I mean, let's use a piece of code from Python called **type()**. This code will tell us the data type of the input we give it. Try typing the following code in your shell:

```
favorite_number = 3
type(favorite_number)
```

What type did the computer tell you **favorite_number** is? Does it say
`<class 'int'>`? Perfect! *Int* is an abbreviation for integer, and it's exactly what we
expect! Now, let's see what happens if you store your favorite number within quotes:

```
favorite_number = "3"
type(favorite_number)
```

What type is it now? A *str*? Oh no! We've tricked the computer into thinking we
were saving a string variable! Whoops. This is why we don't use quotes when working
with integers (or any of the other numeric types we will learn about soon). So remember: we don't need quotes around integers.

GOOD THINGS TO KNOW ABOUT VARIABLES

Variables will be used often in our coding activities. Here are some good practices to
keep in mind whenever you create one:

Variables Cannot Start with a Number

When naming a variable, you want to be as descriptive as possible, but also follow the
rules of Python. One of those rules is that variable names can't start with a number. Try
creating one, and see what happens:

```
100_days_of_code = 100
```

Did you get a syntax error? See, I told you Python doesn't like numbers in variable
names! This is because when the computer starts translating, it immediately sees
the number and assumes the rest of the code will be a number. So, when it finds that
there's more to it and you are actually creating a variable, it gets really confused!

Variables Should Have the Same Styling

There are all kinds of ways to write your variables. The most important thing to remember is to pick one way and stick to it.

As you've seen so far, I write my variables using all lowercase letters, and if I need to
use more than one word to name one, I separate the words using an underscore so it is
easier to read. However, there are other ways to write variables, including:

camelCase: the first word of a variable name is not capitalized, but every other word
after is.

Example: **numberOfCookies**

PascalCase: every word in a variable name is capitalized.

Example: `NumberOfCookies`

There is no naming method that is the "best." Just choose the one that makes the most sense to you and stick to it. Why is this important? The computer doesn't recognize variable names unless they are exactly as you typed them. So, if you suddenly write `FavoriteNumber` instead of `favorite_number`, you will get an error message, as the computer sees this code as two different variables!

>>> **TROUBLESHOOTING TIP:** Why do we connect words or use underscores (_) between words? This is because Python doesn't recognize spaces in variable names. We either have to connect words (nospaceatall or NoSpaceAtAll) or use underscores to connect them (underscores_between_words). If you use spaces, you'll get an error message!

Variables Should Have Meaning

Lastly, variable names should be as descriptive as possible. This means that when you read your code, you should know right away what your variable is and what kind of data it is storing. You should be able to understand it!

Here is a list of good variable names:

- `mood = "happy"`
- `age = 10`
- `favorite_color = "purple"`
- `number_of_books = 4`

And here's a list of not-so-good variable names:

- `a = 5`
- `num_pens = 13`
- `curDay = "Thursday"`
- `fAvOrItE_DrInK = "coffee"`

See the difference? Clear names with meaning and a consistent style are your best bets for great variable names.

We've learned some pretty neat things so far, right? There's so much more we can do, though. Let's get going!

FANCY PRINTING

Now that we know how to use variables, we can use them to do some fancier things with our **print()** function. I'll you show some of them now.

FORMATTED STRING LITERALS

Don't let the term "formatted string literals" scare you off—let me explain. Strings are more useful when we change certain parts of them or move certain parts around. If you remember in our earlier section, most of the strings we printed were full phrases or sentences. We also knew exactly what to print and didn't really need to change it.

But, what if we did need to change it? Let's go back to our example (which I've changed to use double quotes):

```
print("I'm so happy to be learning how to code in Python!")
```

Imagine that, instead of simply being happy to be learning how to code in Python, you're **ecstatic**! Or **overjoyed**! Or **delighted**! How would you change your sentence to the word that describes how you feel about learning how to code in Python?

With formatted string literals!

In Python, we can use formatted string literals, or *f-strings*, to produce formatted strings, which are like normal strings, but set up in a specific way or pattern. Using f-strings gives us an easy way to replace parts of a string or change their order. To do this, we first escape our entire string with the letter *f* and then use special characters known as *braces*, which look like this: **{}**, to do the replacing or reordering. Here's an example:

To use an f-string, you first have to create a variable:

```
food = "cake"
```

Without one, the f-string wouldn't know what to replace! Next, our actual f-string:

```
f"I like {food}"
```

If you coded along in the shell while reading, then you should see this:

```
'I like cake'
```

Here's what's happening: When you use the **f** character before a string, the computer knows that you are about to create an f-string. Once it knows this, it starts looking for the opening and closing quotes of the string like normal, but when it comes across some braces ({}), it says, "Oh, here's a part of the string Human wants me to replace. What does it say? 'food'? Oh! I know that variable! And I know exactly where I stored it! Let me get that real quick . . . Got it! It's actually a tag for 'cake.' Now, let me just put the word 'cake' in there and remove this f-string placeholder. Nice!" Once it finishes replacing all the parts of our string, it outputs the final version to our console window.

Super cool!

So now, back to our earlier question about how to change "happy" to "ecstatic". How do we use f-strings to change our **print()** function? Let's break it down:

Since we know the adjective ("happy") is the only part that will be changing, and will probably be different each time we change it, it's probably a good idea to store it in a variable. Let's do that:

```
feeling = "happy"
```

For now, we created a **feeling** variable and assigned it to "happy", since that's how we currently feel!

Next, we know that our sentence will mostly stay the same, except for the adjective we are using to describe how we feel about coding in Python. So, let's change the parameter in our **print()** function to be an f-string instead:

```
print(f"I'm so {feeling} to be learning how to code in Python!")
```

Great! Now our **print()** function will always print out the current feeling we have about learning Python! :D

Go ahead and save this code in its own file. Once you're done giving it a file name, open it in its own window, change your **feeling** variable to a different adjective, and save your code again. Now run your code (press F5). Do you see your new sentence with your new adjective? Awesome! This will become extremely helpful when we need to start replacing more parts of our strings.

Easier Multi-Line Strings

Remember how we printed multi-line strings earlier in the chapter? There, we used \n escape characters, but the code looked a little funny and kind of hard to read, like this:

```
print("Here is \na sentence \non many \ndifferent lines.")
```

With f-strings, we can make our code a lot cleaner and easier to read. Let's rewrite our multi-line sentence like this:

```
multiline_sentence = """
    Here is
    a sentence
    on many
    different lines.

"""
print(f"{multiline_sentence}")
```

Looks a lot simpler, doesn't it?

Here's what's happening: We create a variable called **multiline_sentence**. We then assign that variable to our actual multi-line sentence, which is typed out exactly as we want it on its different lines. You'll notice that, instead of our normal quotes, we use another special type of escape character for multi-line strings—these are called *triple quotes*. All that means is that we are using a pair of three double quotes or a pair of three single quotes (remember, don't mix and match!) as the starting and ending quotes for our multi-line string. This tells the computer to print out what we put in between these triple quotes exactly the way we have it. After that, we use our handy f-string to print it!

CODE COMPLETE!

Chapter 2 is done! In this chapter, we learned about the **print()** function and some of its quirks. Remember:

- The **print()** function is used to write text output from our code, which can be seen in our shell.

- The **print()** function sometimes has trouble printing certain characters or kinds of text, but we can usually get around that with escape characters.

- We can print **single** or **multi-line** text.

Another important topic we covered is **variables**. These are the tags that hold information for us and are used almost everywhere in programming. We learned:

- Variables can't start with a number.

- Variables should have the same styling, meaning they should use capitalization, underscores, or no spaces consistently.

- Variables should be descriptive and have meaning so we can understand them.

Finally, we learned about fancier ways to print text, specifically by using **f-strings**. We learned:

- F-strings allow us to use variables in our output text.

- F-strings let us print something exactly as we type it, even with multi-line text.

- F-strings make our code a lot cleaner and easier to read.

Get ready—next, we'll dive into numbers, other kinds of numerical types in Python, and operators. But first, check out the following activities that put what we've learned into action!

CHAPTER 2 ★ ACTIVITIES

- -

Now that we've learned what the **print()** function does and why it is one of the most important functions in Python, try these activities!

ACTIVITY 1: INTRODUCE YOURSELF

We're going to be working with the computer a lot and asking it to do a bunch of cool things for us. We might as well introduce ourselves and make friends!

What to Do

Use the **print()** function to introduce yourself to the computer. Your introduction should be seen in the console window (see page 14 for the lesson that will help you do this).

Sample Expected Output

```
"Hi! My name is Adrienne."
```

ACTIVITY 2: TO QUOTE A QUOTE

A quote in non-coding terms is a sentence or short phrase that you want to repeat from a person word for word. You usually see it written like this:

"These are the words you are repeating a.k.a. quoting." —Person Who Said This

What to Do

Find a quote online or use one of your own. It can be about something that inspires you, a funny line from a movie, or even something a family member said. Use the **print()** function to write a proper quote (as shown) in the console window. Remember, in order to print out characters like double quotes, you need to properly escape them with the backslash (\) character (see page 26 for the lesson that will help you do this).

Sample Expected Output

```
"Coding is a superpower! You can do so many cool things with your
imagination and code." —Adrienne Tacke
```

ACTIVITY 3: MOOD IS VARIABLE

Usually, our mood changes every day. One day we might be energetic, and the next day we might be tired. Or, if it's a Friday, many of us are happy! Whatever our mood is, we can use a variable to store it.

What to Do

Use a variable to store the mood you are feeling today. Then, use an f-string and your variable to output how you are feeling today in your console window (see page 33 for the lesson that will help you do this).

Sample Expected Output

```
"Today, I feel curious!"
```

ACTIVITY 4: HAIKU, ABOUT YOU!

Have you ever heard of a haiku? It's a form of Japanese poetry that has three lines. The first and last lines have five syllables, and the second line has seven. A syllable is each part of a word that you say. For example, Py-thon has two syllables: "Py" and "thon."

What to Do

Let's try writing a haiku together and printing it in its correct form! Here's one I wrote as an example:

Adrienne enjoys
Coffee, lots of coding, and
Teaching you Python

Once you have three sentences that match haiku form (see how the first line is five syllables, the second line is seven syllables, and the last line is five syllables?), create a new file and follow the steps to print your haiku to your console window.

Haiku Steps

1. Declare a variable to hold your haiku:

```
haiku = """
    Adrienne enjoys
    Coffee, lots of coding, and
    Teaching you Python
"""
```

2. Start typing your **print()** function: **print(**

3. Type an "f" to start an f-string: **print(f**

4. Type your starting quote: **print(f"**

5. Type in your replacement for the f-string. In this case, it will be our **haiku** variable:

```
print(f"{haiku}
```

6. Almost done! Close your parameter with an ending quote and close your function with an ending parenthesis:

```
print(f"{haiku}")
```

Awesome! You have just written a Japanese poem in Python code using multiple lines. Save your file and then run your code (press F5) to see it output to the console window. Now you're a coder and a poet!

ACTIVITY 5: SILLY STORIES

Have you ever played Mad Libs? It's a funny game in which you ask another person to give you different kinds of words—like colors, numbers, adjectives, and more—to fill in the blanks in a short story that they cannot see. After you are done asking the other person for their word choices, you read the full story back to them, using the words that they gave you! Sometimes, the stories can get really funny!

What to Do

Knowing that you can use f-strings to replace parts of strings, write a program that will output your silly story with words from a friend.

Here are some steps to get you started:

1. Create a new file to hold your silly story program.

2. Create four or five variables of different kinds of words. For example:

```
name = ""
adjective = ""
favorite_snack = ""
number = ""
type_of_tree = ""
```

Notice that we didn't assign anything to our variables yet. This is so you can fill them out later when you ask a friend for some words.

3. Create another variable to hold your silly story. You can use this template or write your own:

```
silly_story = f"""
    Hi, my name is {name}.
    I really like {adjective} {favorite_snack}!
    I like it so much, I try to eat it at least {number} times
    every day.
    It tastes even better when you eat it under a {type_of_tree}!

"""
```

4. Finally, use a **print()** function to output your silly story:

```
print(silly_story)
```

5. That's it! Now, go find a friend and ask them for some words (your variables). Change your variables to the words they give you, save your program, and then run it to see your silly story!

ACTIVITY 6: REUSABLE VARIABLES

Variables can be assigned to other variables. Let's see how we can reuse a variable in this way to write our names without duplicating code.

What to Do

Create a variable to hold your first name:

```
first_name = 'Adrienne'
```

Now, create a second variable called **full_name**. Without typing your first name again, assign your full name to your **full_name** variable using f-strings and your existing **first_name** variable! Print out your **full_name** variable (see page 33 for the lesson that will help you do this).

Sample Expected Output

```
"Adrienne Tacke"
```

ACTIVITY 7: BETTER VARIABLE NAMES

Hey, look—one of the programs our friend has written accidentally got hacked! Someone changed all of their variable names to the following:

```
80 = "Adrienne"
98_cookie_39 = "Chocolate chip cookies"
fIrSt_NAMe = 20
LAST_name = "Blue"
309384 = "Adrienne Tacke"
Hellllooooooooooooo_8392982r = "Software Engineer"
```

Uh-oh. The program will never work with some of those variable names, and the others are just plain bad!

What to Do

Can you change the variables to something that won't give errors and is more consistent and descriptive? Once you do, use an f-string to print out all of your variables to make sure they work (see page 33 for the lesson that will help you do this).

Sample Expected Output

```
"Adrienne Chocolate chip cookies 20 Blue Adrienne Tacke Software Engineer"
```

CHALLENGE 1: MULTILAYER CAKE

Let's bake a cake! An electronic one made of characters, anyway. Here are some examples:

```
      (0)                 @@@@          [**]
     (000)               {    }         [*****]
    (00000)             @@@@@@@          [*******]
   (0000000)           {        }
  (000000000)         @@@@@@@@@@@
                     {           }
```

Using what you know about multi-line strings, f-strings, and variables, write a program to print out your electronic cake!

PRINT("HELLO!")

FUN WITH NUMBERS

Along with strings, *numeric types* are another important building block in coding. They help us count objects, perform math operations, keep track of things, and so much more. Knowing all of the different numeric types, what you can do with them, and how to do it will be very important as you move on to the later chapters. Don't worry, you can do this. Let's get started!

NUMERIC TYPES

There are two main numeric types that we'll be using in Python: integers and floats. The first one is one that you're already familiar with and will use most of the time. These are integers, which are the whole numbers (positive or negative) that we are used to. Even though we won't use the other numeric type as much, it's still a good idea to know what it is. Let's talk about floats briefly.

FLOATS

Floating point numbers, or simply *floats*, are numbers that can have whole and fractional parts and are written using decimal points.

```
my_gpa = 3.47
```

Even though these look like decimal numbers, they are not completely the same. This numeric type is used when we need precise calculations, which happens most often in math and science. We actually have a built-in module in Python called the decimal module, which is based on the float type. The big difference is that the decimal module was written with some helpers from the Python language that give it two benefits: First, the helpers make the decimal module faster to use; and second, the decimal module gives us numbers to work with that are closer to what we are used to seeing as humans. We also use the decimal module when we want to deal with money or any type of currency calculations.

OPERATORS

You already learned about integers when we played around with variables, so you're ahead of the game! Now, let's see how we can use integers with operators.

In programming, **operators** are special symbols or keywords that represent an action. They are usually used with **operands**, which are the values you are performing the action on. In this section, our operands will be numbers. If you've ever used a calculator, then you should be familiar with a set of operators that are specifically used for math. These are called **arithmetic operators**.

ARITHMETIC OPERATORS

Also known as the math operators, arithmetic operators are used to perform the basic functions of math. As you'll see in the following chart, most arithmetic operators work just like they do in regular mathematics, with a few exceptions:

Operator Symbol	Operator Name	Action Taken	Examples	Resulting Output
+	Addition	Adds values together	4 + 5	9
–	Subtraction	Subtracts one value from another	10 - 5 5 - 10	5 -5
*	Multiplication	Multiplies values together	9 * 6	54
/	Division	Divides one value by another (answer will always be a float type)	8 / 4 9 / 4	2.0 2.25
%	Modulus	Divides one value by another, and returns the remainder	12 % 5 12 % 6	2 0
//	Floor Division	Divides one value by another, returns the answer rounded to the next smallest whole number	4 // 3 4 // 2	1 2
**	Exponentiation	Raises one value to the power of another	2 ** 5	32

To see these operations in action, go ahead and set the following variables in your shell:

```
a = 6
b = 3
```

CODING FOR KIDS : PYTHON

Now you can begin using different operators on these variables directly in your shell. Try out a few, like these:

a + b
b ** a
a % b

Cool, right? Now, to really get comfortable with them, try out all of the combinations and see what happens! You can check the answers on the following chart, although I think the computer is pretty good at math ;)

Here are all the possible answers that can occur using the different operators and the variables:

Operator Combination	Answer	Operator Combination	Answer
a + b	9	a + a	12
b + a	9	a - a	0
a - b	3	a * a	36
b - a	-3	a / a	1.0
a * b	18	a % a	0
b * a	18	a // a	1
a / b	2.0	a ** a	46656
b / a	0.5	b + b	6
a % b	0	b - b	0
b % a	3	b * b	9
a // b	2	b / b	1.0
b // a	0	b % b	0
a ** b	216	b // b	1
b ** a	729	b ** b	27

FUN WITH NUMBERS

ORDER OF OPERATIONS

A special set of rules are followed for arithmetic operators. This set of rules is called the *order of operations*. It is the proper order in which arithmetic operations should be calculated, especially if you use more than one in a single line of code. Let's say you have many calculations for a single variable, similar to how totals are calculated when we pay for dinner at a restaurant:

```
total = 20 + (20 * .0825) - 1.5 + 3
```

Here, it looks like there's some sales tax (the multiplication) added to our price (first addition calculation), a coupon (the subtraction), and a tip for the waiter (the second addition calculation). What would the total be in this set of calculations? Let's follow the order of operations—here's how:

1. Parentheses

In calculations like this, the computer always calculates any expression in parentheses first. Parentheses tell us "I'm most important" in the *rules of precedence* in math. So in our example, we would calculate the sales tax first (the .0825 represents sales tax of 8.25 percent). In this calculation, 20 * .0825 would equal 1.65 (or technically, 1.6500000000000001 if you code the equation, but we won't get that picky!).

2. Exponentiation

The next calculation that is performed is *exponentiation*. When the computer sees the ** operator, it raises one number to the power of another. What this means is, if you type 2 ** 4 in your shell, you'll get 16, because 2 to the power of 4 (also 2 x 2 x 2 x 2) equals 16. Because our dinner calculation does not have any exponentiation calculations, we move onto the next operation of importance.

3. Multiplication and Division

In the order of operations, multiplication and division are next. They have the same level of importance as each other, so if both a multiplication and division calculation appear in the same line, we start with the calculation on the left and work our way to the right. For example, in this calculation:

```
4 * 3 / 2
```

We would first calculate **4 * 3** (which would be 12), since it's the calculation at the very left. Then, we would calculate the resulting **12 / 2**, since we have worked our way to the right. The final answer would be 6.

Since our dinner calculation does not have any other multiplication or division calculations (except for the one we already calculated in the parentheses step), we can move to the next rule of importance.

HELPFUL HACKS: PEMDAS

Sometimes, it's hard to remember the proper order in which computers make calculations, and you might not always have this book in your hand to refer to. Luckily, we can borrow an acronym from mathematics that stands for the order of operations. It's called **PEMDAS** and is a helpful way to remember the order of operations. Each letter stands for a specific operation, and they are ordered from most important (the left-most letter) to least important (the right-most letter).

So, PEMDAS stands for:

Parentheses
Exponentiation
Multiplication
Division
Addition
Subtraction

The next time you need help remembering the correct order of operations, use the PEMDAS acronym to refresh your memory!

4. Addition and Subtraction

The calculations with the least importance are addition and subtraction. This means they are performed last. So far, our total dinner bill now looks like this, with the sales tax calculated first because it was in parentheses:

```
total = 20 + 1.65 - 1.5 + 3
```

Now, we're left with a quite a few addition and subtraction calculations. Since addition and subtraction have the same level of importance, we use the left-to-right order of calculating them, just like we did with multiplication and division. Let's see the remaining steps:

First add 20 to 1.65	**21.65**
Next, subtract the 1.5 from 21.65	**20.15**
Finally, add the last calculation of 3 to 20.15	**23.15**

That's it! Our total is 23.15 after following the order of operations. Keep in mind, all the steps above aren't actually going to show in your shell. We simply went through the same steps that the computer takes to see how it calculates things!

COMPARISON OPERATORS

The next set of operators we use in programming are called *comparison operators*. Just like their name, comparison operators help us compare one value to another. When we use comparison operators, they give us back a **True** or **False** answer known as a *Boolean type*. Comparison operators and Booleans are super important because they help us make decisions in our code.

There are six main comparison operators, and they are pretty simple to understand. Let's talk about each one:

Greater Than

The *greater-than operator* looks like this: **>**.

When you use it, the computer decides whether the value on the left side of the **>** symbol is larger than the value on the right side of the **>** symbol. For example:

```
3 > 7
```

When you write this code, the computer says, "Hmm, Human wants me to figure something out. Let's see. Is 3 greater than 7? Um, absolutely not! Better tell Human that this is **False**!"

Go ahead and type that code into your shell. What does it tell you? Did it say **False**? That's correct! Just as the computer correctly calculated, 3 is obviously not larger than 7. That's why it returned the verdict of **False**. Easy, right?

Less Than

The *less-than operator* looks like this: **<**

This time, we are figuring out if the value on the left of the **<** symbol is less than, or smaller, than the value on the right side of the **<** symbol. Let's try running our code with this operator to see what happens:

```
3 < 7
```

What does your shell say? Does it say **True**? Awesome! That's obviously correct, because 3 is less than 7!

Greater Than or Equal To

Okay, here's what the *greater-than-or-equal-to operator* looks like: **>=**

We're already familiar with the first symbol, so let's talk about the second symbol. We've used the equal sign (=) before to assign pieces of data to variables (remember **mood = happy**?). When we use it as an operator, though, we are deciding, in part, if the value on the left of the **>=** operator is equal to the value on the right of the **>=** operator.

But this operator is special.

Because there are two symbols in this operator, we are trying to decide if the value on left of the **>=** operator is **greater than** the one on the right *or* if the value on the left is the **same as** the value on the right. Only *one* of these cases needs to be true in order for the computer to decide that the entire expression is **True**. So, in code:

```
4 >= 3
```

What do you think this will return? **True** or **False**?

Did you say **True**? You're right! Because 4 is greater than 3, we know that the greater-than operator is correct. So even though the second operator, the equal-to operator, is not correct (because 4 is obviously not the same as 3), the computer still returns **True** because at least one operator is correct (the greater-than action).

How about this?

```
3 >= 3
```

This one is also **True**! This time, the equal-to operator is correct, instead of the greater-than operator.

Here's one more:

```
1 >= 3
```

What do you think? **False**? That's right! Both operators are not correct. The number 1 is not greater than 3, so the greater-than operator is incorrect, and 1 is not the same as 3, which also makes the equal-to operator incorrect. Because both operators are not right, the computer's final decision for this is **False**. Great job!

Less Than or Equal To

Starting to see a pattern here? :)

This is the *less-than-or-equal-to operator*. **<=**

Just like the greater-than-or-equal-to operator, we are making sure at least one of the operators is correct. For the less-than-or-equal-to operator, we are looking at the values to see if the value on the left of the **<=** operator is *either* smaller than the one on the right of the **<=** operator *or* the same as the one on the right.

What do you think this code will return when you write it in your shell?

```
1 <= 3
```

That's right! This returns **True** because 1 is smaller than 3. This makes the less-than operator correct, even if the equal-to operator isn't. And since one of the operators is correct, the whole thing returns **True**.

How about this expression?

```
8 <= 8
```

Yup, same thing. This also returns **True**, as the equal-to operator is correct.

Not too bad, right?

Equal To

Almost done, promise!

This is the *equal-to operator*. **==**

This one is much simpler than the last two operators. Just like it sounds, it asks the computer to decide if the value on the left of the **==** symbol is the same as the value on the right of the **==** symbol. Easy!

How will this return?

```
23 == 22
```

False!

What about this one?

```
10 == 10
```

True!

Here's a tricky one:

```
10 == "10"
```

What do you think? Did you guess **False**? You're right! If you guessed **True**, that's okay, too. This one is a tricky one, but I'll make sure you aren't tricked again!

Here's what's happening: When we use the **equal-to** operator, we are asking the computer to decide if the values on the left and right of the **==** symbol are the same. Though it looks the same to us, this is what the computer figures out:

"Hmm, here's another expression Human wants me to figure out. Let's see, is 10 equal to "10"? Ha! That's a clever one! It is **False**! The value on the left is the number 10, which is an integer type. The value on the right is also 10, but it is a string type (the quotes tell me that). This means that the values aren't really the same, because an integer type is never the same as a string type! Sorry, Human, but the answer is **False**!"

That's okay, computer. That's actually a very smart decision. Think about it: Do *we* think of text and numbers as the same thing? Text can sometimes look like or be numbers (just like most of the examples we've gone through in this chapter), but can you do any calculations with text? Not really. You wouldn't add the number 20 to the word "cookies," right? What would that answer even be?!

This is why the computer also doesn't see integer and string types as the same types. So when we use the equal-to operator, remember that the computer will check that the values are the same type and the same value/number/text.

Not Equal To

Last one! You're so awesome for making it this far!

Here's the *not-equal-to operator*: **!=**

Also like the name, the not-equal-to operator asks the computer to figure out if the value on the left side of the `!=` symbol is *not* the same as the value on the right side of the `!=` symbol. Go ahead and try to guess the next few examples before writing the code in your shell:

1. `5 != "five"`

2. `10 != "10"`

3. `4 != 3`

4. `9 != 9`

Did you guess correctly? Let's go over each example now!

1. The first expression is **True**. Remember, it's asking if the two values are not the same. This is **True**. It's a little tricky, but I wanted to remind you of the importance of comparing different types. So, even though our mind is telling us there's a number, or integer type, of 5 on the left, and the word, or string type, of "five" on the right, the computer will still return **True**. Why? Because an integer type is not the same as a string type. And since the not-equal-to operator is deciding exactly that, the expression is **True**!

2. The next example is also **True**. Even though they look like the same number, the value on the right is still a string type! So, just as before, the computer sees "Is this integer type 10 not the same as this string type '10'"? And since they are not the same type, this returns **True**.

HELPFUL HACKS: PYTHON'S MATH MODULE

Since there are many common math calculations and concepts, Python has created a special *module*, or prewritten code, that's ready for us to use called the math module. It has functions that can do things for you, like exponentiation or addition calculations, and others that give you back special numbers in math (like pi).

Be sure to check out all of the functions the math module has to offer in the resources section (see page 214), and see how you can use them in the later chapters!

CODING FOR KIDS : PYTHON

3. The third example is also **True**. This one should be a little more straightforward and not as tricky. We can clearly see that the number 4 is not the same as the number 3. So this is **True**.

4. Finally, the last example is **False**! We see that the value on the left, which is the number 9, is also the value on the right, another number 9. But because we are using the not-equal-to operator, we are asking the computer, "Is this integer type 9 *not* the same as this integer type 9?" And, of course, the computer tells us, "Actually, they are the same, so this expression is **False**." So this should return **False** in your shell.

LOGICAL OPERATORS

Logical operators are used to help us compare **True** or **False** operands. These are very helpful because they can make our decision-making rules more complex, which means smarter code! There are three main logical operators: and, or, and not. Let's see what each can do.

and

The *and operator* checks that the values on the right and left of it are both **True**. It looks like this: **and**

If there's a point in our code that should only run when two conditions are met, we should use the **and** operator. Imagine that you're going through a pizza buffet and you need to pick only the slices of pizza that you like. You like pepperoni and you like mushrooms, and you'd love to pick up a slice or two of that kind of pizza if it had both of those toppings.

While walking around, you sadly see that there's only a pizza with pepperoni but no mushrooms. Let's say we had variables that held this information:

```
pizza_has_pepperoni = True
pizza_has_mushrooms = False
```

To check that the pizza you were evaluating had both pepperoni and mushrooms, you'd use the **and** operator like this:

```
pizza_has_pepperoni and pizza_has_mushrooms True
```

The **and** operator allows you to check both conditions: that the pizza slice has pepperoni *and* that it has mushrooms. Only then would you take a slice of pizza, if both conditions were met! Unfortunately, you won't be taking a slice, since only one condition is **True**. :(

or

The *or operator* checks to make sure that at least one value being compared is **True**.
It looks like this: **or**
Going back to our pizza example, let's say that you couldn't find any pizza that had both pepperoni and mushroom on it (bummer). Still wanting pizza, you decide that if the pizza has either pepperoni *or* mushroom on it, you'll select that pizza. Here is where the or operator will come in handy. To check for either pepperoni *or* mushroom, you'd write code like this:

```
pizza_has_pepperoni or pizza_has_mushrooms
```

That way, if the pizza you were checking had either pepperoni *or* mushroom on it, you'd take it.

not

The *not operator* checks to make sure that the value being compared is **False**.
It looks like this: **not**
Just as you'd take any pizza that had pepperoni or mushroom on it, you definitely would not take any that had onions on it. Let's say we had a variable called **pizza_has_onions** and its value was **True**. To make sure you don't get any pizza with onions on it, you could use the **not** operator:

```
not pizza_has_onion
```

It looks a little funny if you try to read it out loud, but it is correct! You're basically saying, "Hey, computer, make sure that the fact of the pizza having onions is *not true*."

CODE COMPLETE!

Chapter 3 introduced us to numbers and the interesting things we can do with them.

- There are two main numeric types we will work with most often: **integers** and **floats**.

- Operators are special keywords or characters that enable us to perform actions. The first set we learned about were **arithmetic operators**.

- Arithmetic operators are similar to the ones we use in math.

- When working with arithmetic operators, it is important to remember the order of operations to calculate something correctly.

- The order of operations, from most important to least important, is: parentheses, exponentiation, multiplication, division, addition, and subtraction (PEMDAS).

- If there is more than one calculation with the same level of importance to evaluate, we go from left to right.

Another set of operators we learned about are **comparison operators**. These help us compare two values to each other.

- We have operators to compare if one value is greater than (>), less than (<), greater than or equal to (>=), less than or equal to (<=), equal to (==), and not equal to (!=) another.

Finally, we learned about **logical operators**, which help us make smarter comparisons.

- The **and operator** helps us determine if two expressions are both **True**.

- The **or operator** checks that at least one expression we pass to it is **True**.

- The **not operator** determines if the expression we pass to it is **False**.

Next up, we'll learn about more things we can do with strings and some new types!

CHAPTER 3 ★ ACTIVITIES

ACTIVITY 1: HOW OLD ARE YOU?

So, we've introduced ourselves to the computer. Now, let's add to our introduction and tell it how old we are.

What to Do

Change your existing **print()** function (the one where you introduced yourself to the computer) to use an f-string (see page 33 for the lesson that will help you do this). Create two variables: one called **name** and one called **age**. Assign a string with your name to the **name** variable. Assign a math operation (that equals your age) to the **age** variable. For example:

```
age = 20 + 7
```

Finally, print out your new introduction to the computer using your f-string and **name** and **age** variables!

Sample Expected Output

`"Hi! My name is Adrienne and I am 27 years old!"`

ACTIVITY 2: OPERATION PEMDAS

Just like math, the arithmetic operators follow a special order to make calculations. Let's see if you can create a super calculation using this knowledge!

What to Do

Create a variable called **magic_number**. Then, assign to it a special calculation that equals 333 (see page 44 for the lesson that will help you do this). The calculation must follow these rules:

- You must use the ** operator at least once.

- You must use the % operator at least once.

Once you've assigned your **magic_number** variable to your calculation, use the **print()** function to make sure it equals 333!

ACTIVITY 3: COOKIE COMPARISONS

Say you and your friends are eating some chocolate chip cookies. While you are all happily snacking away, one of your friends says, "My chocolate chip cookie has the most chocolate chips!" You think to yourself, "I think mine does." And now your other friends are curious, and look down at their chocolate chip cookies to see how their cookies compare with their friends'. How can you use coding to confirm whose claim is **True**? Who has more or less chocolate chips in their cookie between you and your friend; and how about among your other friends?

We could write a small program to help us make that decision. Let's do it!

Imagine that we built an awesome machine that was able to scan some cookies and then give you variables with the number of chocolate chips each contained. How would you use comparison operators to help you decide?

What to Do

For each pair of friends, write a **print()** function that outputs the two friends' chocolate chip numbers, the comparison you are using, and if it is **True**. Here is an example:

Dolores and Teddy both have cookies. Teddy thinks his cookie has more chocolate chips than Dolores's cookie. Of course, Dolores thinks the opposite. Let's see who is right.

Beep boop scanning noise

Great! We've scanned their cookies, and this is what is given to us by our cookie scanning machine:

```
dolores_chocolate_chips = 13
teddy_chocolate_chips = 9
```

Teddy thinks he has more chocolate chips in his cookie than Dolores does in hers. How would we write that comparison in code?

```
teddy_chocolate_chips > dolores_chocolate_chips
```

Exactly! Teddy thinks he has more chocolate chips than Dolores, so we use the greater-than operator (>). Now, how would we print out the results of this chocolate chip battle, including the comparison we are making? Hint: We can use f-strings! And another hint: full code comparisons can be used in the same way as variables!

```
print(f"Teddy's cookie has more chocolate chips than Dolores's. This
is {teddy_chocolate_chips > dolores_chocolate_chips}!")
```

Awesome! It's kind of long, but it works!

Here are some more friends you need to help! Write a similar **print()** function for each pair of friends and their claim:

Rey and Finn

Rey says she has less than or equal to the number of chocolate chips as Finn.

```
rey_chocolate_chips = 10
finn_chocolate_chips = 18
```

Tom and Jerry

Tom says he does not have the same amount of chocolate chips in his cookie as Jerry.

```
tom_chocolate_chips = 50
jerry_chocolate_chips = "50"
```

Trinity and Neo

Neo says he has the same number of chocolate chips as Trinity.

```
neo_chocolate_chips = 3
trinity_chocolate_chips = 3
```

Gigi and Kiki

Kiki says she has less chocolate chips in her cookie than Gigi.

```
kiki_chocolate_chips = 30
gigi_chocolate_chips = 31
```

Bernard and Elsie

Bernard says he has at least the same amount of chocolate chips as Elsie, maybe even more!

```
bernard_chocolate_chips = 1010
elsie_chocolate_chips = 10101
```

ACTIVITY 4: PIE PARTY!

Today's our lucky day. We get to help the best baker in town prepare for the pie party! Baker Miguel wants to know how many of each kind of pie to bake to make sure everyone gets a slice that they like. We have some information available, but you'll have to write some code to figure out exactly how many pies, and which pies, to bake!

Here's the information we know:

```
total_people = 124
graham_cracker_crust_lovers = 40
vanilla_wafer_crust_lovers = 64
oreo_crust_lovers = 20
```

Pie Types

Chocolate and Caramel Pie
```
pie_crust = "graham cracker"
pie_slices = 10
```

Triple Berry Pie
```
pie_crust = "vanilla wafer"
pie_slices = 12
```

Pumpkin Pie
```
pie_crust = "graham cracker"
pie_slices = 12
```

Apple Pie
```
pie_crust = "vanilla wafer"
pie_slices = 10
```

Banana Cream Pie

```
pie_crust = "vanilla wafer"
pie_slices = 10
```

Mango Pie

```
pie_crust = "graham cracker"
pie_slices = 12
```

S'mores Pie

```
pie_crust = "oreo"
pie_slices = 12
```

What to Do

Using logical operators, the **print()** function, and f-strings, write some code for each type of pie that determines if you can evenly divide the number of slices that type of pie has by the total number of people in that particular crust lovers' group!

Sample Expected Output

`'The Chocolate and Caramel pie can be evenly divided for all Graham Crust Lovers? True'`

ACTIVITY 5: OUTFIT CHECKER

Cher and Dionne are about to go to a fancy party. Being the fashionistas they are, they want to make sure their outfits aren't the same, but a few things in common are okay, especially since they both love pink! Let's write some code to make sure their outfits are as individual as they are!

What to Do

Using the variables provided, your knowledge of the **print()** function, and the proper logical operators, write code to help you check Cher and Dionne's outfits! Here are some variables that describe each girl's outfit:

```
cher_dress_color = 'pink'
cher_shoe_color = 'white'
cher_has_earrings = True
dionne_dress_color = 'purple'
dionne_shoe_color = 'pink'
dionne_has_earrings = True
```

For each outfit check, first determine which variables to use that best match the scenario. Then, write some code to compare the variables you have chosen with the proper logical operator. Finally, use the **print()** function to print a sentence stating the outfit check and use your comparison code as a **True** or **False** answer.

Example Outfit Check
At least one person is wearing purple.
Best matching variables to use for this outfit check:

```
cher_dress_color, dionne_dress_color
```

Choose a logical operator that allows you to test the condition in the outfit check. For this one, we only need to make sure that at least one person is wearing purple (at least one expression was **True**), so using the **or** operator is probably best.

Finally, use that comparison code to print the answer to the outfit check!

```
print(f"At least one person is wearing purple? {code to check that
either cher or dionne's dress is purple}")
```

Example Output:
```
At least one person is wearing purple? True
```

Outfit Check 1
Cher and Dionne have different dress colors.

Outfit Check 2
Cher and Dionne are both wearing earrings.

Outfit Check 3
At least one person is wearing pink.

Outfit Check 4
No one is wearing green.

Outfit Check 5
Cher and Dionne have the same shoe color.

Sample Expected Output

```
Cher and Dionne have matching dress colors? False
Someone is wearing pink? True
```

ACTIVITY 6: LOGICAL LAB!

We've learned about the three sets of operators used in Python: arithmetic, logical, and comparison. This will come in handy now, because Ada needs our help sorting through her lab materials.

What to Do

Create a new file called adas-materials-report and save it. Then, declare the following variables:

```
beakers = 20
tubes = 30
rubber_gloves = 10
safety_glasses = 4
```

Ada has three friends coming to her lab to help her out, so you'll need to determine if there are enough materials for each friend. To safely run some experiments, each friend needs to have:

1 pair of safety glasses
2 rubber gloves
5 beakers
10 tubes

Knowing this, create new variables to hold a Boolean value (**True** or **False**) determining if there are enough items for all the scientists:

```
enough_safety_glasses = <Write some code here!>
enough_rubber_gloves = <Write some code here!>
enough_tubes = <Write some code here!>
enough_beakers = <Write some code here!>
```

61

FUN WITH NUMBERS

In the placeholders that say **<Write some code here!>**, write code that uses different arithmetic operators to first figure out if each friend will receive the proper amount of materials. Next, combine that code with some comparison operators to result in either a **True** or **False** answer. This will be the Boolean you assign to your "enough lab materials" variables.

Finally, once you have Booleans assigned to your variables, use them with logical operators to determine the following scenarios:

- There are enough gloves and safety glasses for each girl.

- There are enough tubes or enough beakers for each girl.

- Each girl has enough safety glasses and beakers or enough tubes and beakers.

- Each girl has enough gloves, safety glasses, tubes, and beakers.

For example, in the first scenario, "There are enough gloves and safety glasses for each girl," we can use the **enough_rubber_gloves** and **enough_safety_glasses** variables for comparison with the *and* operator to check for the scenario's conditions.

Put all of this information together in a **final_report** variable:

```
final_report = f'''

    Here is the final report for lab materials:
    -
    Each girl has enough safety glasses: {add the right variable here}
    Each girl has enough rubber gloves: {add the right variable here}
    Each girl has enough tubes: {add the right variable here}
    Each girl has enough beakers: {add the right variable here}
    -
    There are enough gloves and safety glasses for each girl: {write
    some code here}
    There are enough tubes and or enough beakers for each girl: {write
    some code here}
    Each girl has enough safety glasses and beakers or enough tubes and
    beakers: {write some code here}
    Each girl has enough gloves, safety glasses, tubes, and beakers:
    {write some code here}

'''
```

Use this variable in your **print()** function (be sure to fill in the blanks with the information you figured out above) to see the results!

ACTIVITY 7: MODULUS MATH

What to Do

Practice using the *modulus* operator (see the chart on page 44) to write some code that calculates the modulus of numbers that can't be evenly divided. Print the remaining number the modulus operator gives back for these numbers.

Example: **12345 % 88**

ACTIVITY 8: PLANETARY EXPONENTIATION

Scientist Angie needs our help! She's been exploring other galaxies and has been comparing how many planets they have to the nine that we have in our solar system (because even though it's a dwarf planet, she wants to include Pluto). Can you write some code to help her calculate the total planets for the other galaxies?

What to Do

Use the exponentiation operator to print out the total number of planets the other galaxies have. To do this, take our total number of planets and raise it to the power of each galaxy's magic number. Be sure to use the **total_planets** variable provided for your calculations!

```
total_planets = 9
```

Example Galaxy

In the Pentatopia galaxy, their magic number is 5. Write a **print()** function that prints out how many planets the Pentatopia galaxy has!

Sample Code

```
print(f"The Pentatopia galaxy has {write code to calculate what 9 to
the power of 5 is} planets!")
```

Sample Output

```
The Pentatopia galaxy has 59049 planets!
```

In the **Tripolia galaxy**, their magic number is 3. Write a **print()** function that prints out how many planets the Tripolia galaxy has.

In the **Deka galaxy**, their magic number is 10. Write a **print()** function that prints out how many planets the Deka galaxy has.

In the **Heptaton galaxy**, their magic number is 7. Write a **print()** function that prints out how many planets the Heptaton galaxy has.

In the **Oktopia galaxy**, their magic number is 8. Write a **print()** function that prints out how many planets the Oktopia galaxy has.

CHAPTER 3 ★ CHALLENGES

CHALLENGE 1: DINNER DECISIONS

Imagine that we are at a buffet, where we are given many different options of food to choose from. There's a noodle station and a pizza station and all kinds of other stations that serve different cuisines. And then, there's the most important station: the dessert station. Unfortunately, the names of all the different dishes have been mixed up, so we can't be sure that what we're picking is actually the food we think it is!

If we were to write a program to pick different foods for us from the buffet, using only these name cards, how would we make sure that only the foods we want are chosen?

What to Do

Using our Silly Stories program from chapter 2 as a guide (page 38), let's create another program to decide our what to eat for dinner.

Create variables for your name and the different parts of your dinner, filling in each with your choices:

```
name = ""
entree = ""
side_one = ""
side_two = ""
dessert_one = ""
dessert_two = ""
dessert_three = ""
```

CODING FOR KIDS : PYTHON

Create another variable to hold your dinner choices. You can use this template or write your own!

```
dinner_decisions = f"""
    Hi, my name is {name}.
    I chose {entree} as my main meal!
    To go with it, I chose {side_one} and {side_two} as my sides.
    And the best part, I have {dessert_one}, {dessert_two}, and
    {dessert_three} waiting for me for dessert!
    Let's eat!
"""
```

For each variable, make some decisions about your meal by checking the following variables and seeing if they actually contain the food you want to eat. If they do, assign that to your dinner variables.

Buffet Option Name Cards

Entrees
```
pepperoni_pizza = "91334"
hamburger = "cheeseburger"
steak = "0980sdf3"
pasta = "ribs"
fried_chicken = "fried chicken"
```

Sides
```
baked_potato = "mashed potatoes"
mashed_potatoes = "baked potato"
french_fries = "french fries"
mac_n_cheese = "33333"
steamed_carrots = "green"
broccoli = "chocolate chips"
```

Desserts
```
chocolate_ice_cream = "chocolate ice cream"
strawberry_ice_cream = "vanilla ice cream"
apple_pie = "pumpkin pie"
egg_pie = "302948"
watermelon = "oranges"
vanilla_donut = "cereal"
```

After using some logical operators to make your choices, use a **print()** function to output your final meal:

```
print(dinner_decisions)
```

That's it! Save your program, run it, and see what dinner you ended up choosing!

STRINGS AND OTHER THINGS

STRINGS + OPERATORS

In the last chapter, we learned about operators and how we use them with numeric types. Did you know that we can use some of them with strings, too? Let's see how!

CONCATENATING STRINGS

Concatenation, a fancy word that means putting things together, is one thing we can do with strings! This is done using the addition (+) operator. We know that when we use this operator with numbers, it will add them together. What do you think will happen when we add two characters or words together? Try it out:

```
print("basket" + "ball")
```

Interesting! We have created the new string "basketball" by adding two separate strings, "basket" and "ball," together.

Here's what's happening: When the computer sees the addition (+) operator, it says, "Okay, Human wants me to add some values here. Let's see what the values are." Then, when it sees that you are trying to add two strings together, it says, "Well, you can't really add two strings in the same way you would add two integers. So I'll put these two strings together and give it back to Human as a single string." How logical! That's exactly how "adding" two strings would work.

Interestingly enough, you have probably encountered concatenation before without even realizing it! Have you ever filled out a form with a section for "First Name" and a separate section for "Last Name"? Well, the coders who created that form probably used concatenation to show your full name after you submit the form. It's very useful and not at all difficult to do. Let's try it out!

First, we need a place to store our first name and last name. Were you thinking variables? Because that's the right way to start!

```
first_name = "Adrienne"
last_name = "Tacke"
```

Now that we have our first and last names stored, how would we print them out as a full name? As we'll see more and more in coding, there is always more than one way to do something! We could use the addition operator directly in our **print()** function:

```
print(first_name + last_name)
```

Or, we could create another variable to hold the full name and print that instead:

```
full_name = first_name + last_name
print(full_name)
```

Did you notice anything funny when executing this code, though? Your name probably printed out a little *too* combined and close together, like this:

```
Python 3.7.0 Shell                                                    —   □   ✕

File  Edit  Shell  Debug  Options  Window  Help
Python 3.7.0 (v3.7.0:1bf9cc5093, Jun 27 2018, 04:59:51) [MSC v.1914 64 bit (AMD6
4)] on win32
Type "copyright", "credits" or "license()" for more information.
>>> first_name = "Adrienne"
>>> last_name = "Tacke"
>>> full_name = first_name + last_name
>>> print(full_name)
AdrienneTacke
>>>
```

Remember, the computer will do *exactly* what you want it to, and in this case, it added our **first_name** and **last_name** variables together exactly as it should! If we want to print our name out the way we normally see a full name, we need to be exact and add the space between our names. Again, we can do this in several ways:

We could concatenate an actual space in between our **first_name** and **last_name**:

```
full_name = first_name + " " + last_name
print(full_name)
```

Or, we could add the space after our first name:

```
first_name = "Adrienne "
```

Or before our last name:

```
last_name = " Tacke"
```

That way, when we print out our concatenated name, it will include the space.

```
full_name = first_name + last_name
print(full_name)
```

Can you think of other ways to print out your full name properly?

3 + "Cookies" = A Confused Computer

What happens when we add integers and strings? Can we even do that? Try the following code:

```
print(3 + "Cookies")
```

Were you able to print out this concatenated string? Probably not, but that's expected.

Here's what's happening: Just like before, the computer sees your addition operator and knows that you'd like to add some values together. But when it sees that one value is an integer and the other as a string, it says, "Hmm, integers and strings don't really 'add' together, so I'm not sure what Human is asking me to do. Better let them know I don't understand their code." And here, you get your first *type error* (**TypeError**), which is the computer's way of telling you that it can't do something you are asking it to do because of a data type issue.

MULTIPLYING STRINGS (WHAT?!)

Yeah, you read that right. In Python, we can also use the multiplication (*) operator with strings! What would this look like? Try this:

```
print(5 * "balloon!")
```

Did you excitedly give your shell five balloons (as in the text "balloon!" printed five times)?

Neat! How nice of you! As we've seen, the multiplication (*) operator works similarly with strings as it does with integers. Instead of multiplying an integer a specific number of times, it multiplies the exact string you give it.

LISTS

One of the most useful data types in Python is lists. A *list* is exactly what it sounds like: a list or collection of objects. Lists are very useful because they allow us to work with a lot of data at the same time, which is something we do very often in programming. In code, we create a list by giving it a name and assigning it to a collection of objects we would like it to hold. This collection of objects is stored in between **brackets**, which look like this: **[ ]**, and the objects are separated by commas. When working with string objects, be sure to place each object within single quotes! Here's a list holding a collection of my favorite desserts:

```python
my_favorite_desserts = ['Cookies', 'Cake', 'Ice Cream', 'Donuts']
```

Lists can hold all kinds of things. We can create a list of strings, like this one:

```python
citrus_fruits = ['Orange', 'Lemon', 'Grapefruit', 'Pomelo', 'Lime']
```

Or a list of integers:

```python
bunnies_spotted = [3, 5, 2, 8, 4, 5, 4, 3, 3]
```

Even a list of Booleans:

```python
robot_answers = [True, False, False, True, True]
```

What's even cooler is that lists don't *always* have to be the same data type. You can have a list of mixed objects as well:

```python
facts_about_adrienne = ['Adrienne', 'Tacke', 27, True]
```

Having this kind of flexibility is one reason lists are so useful. But wait, there's more! There are several other interesting features about lists that make them useful. Let's talk about each one!

LISTS ARE ORDERED

When we create a list, we are storing not only a collection of objects, but their order as well. This is important because it affects how we change the list, how we access a list's objects, and how we compare it with other lists. To see the importance of a list's order, try the following code:

```python
citrus_fruits = ['Orange', 'Lemon', 'Grapefruit', 'Pomelo', 'Lime']
more_citrus_fruits = ['Orange', 'Grapefruit', 'Lemon', 'Pomelo', 'Lime']
citrus_fruits == more_citrus_fruits
```

What happens? Are they equal lists?

```
Python 3.7.0 Shell                                            —    □    ×

File  Edit  Shell  Debug  Options  Window  Help
Python 3.7.0 (v3.7.0:1bf9cc5093, Jun 27 2018, 04:59:51) [MSC v.1914 64 bit (AMD6 ^
4)] on win32
Type "copyright", "credits" or "license()" for more information.
>>> citrus_fruits = ['Orange', 'Lemon', 'Grapefruit', 'Pomelo', 'Lime']
>>> more_citrus_fruits = ['Orange', 'Grapefruit', 'Lemon', 'Pomelo', 'Lime']
>>> citrus_fruits == more_citrus_fruits
False
```

Nope!

Here's what's happening: As we learned in chapter 2, the computer knows that we want to compare two values when we use the **==** operator. When it looks at the first value, it says, "Okay, so we have a list of **citrus_fruits** here. It has an **Orange, Lemon, Grapefruit, Pomelo,** and **Lime** stored in it." It then checks the other value we are comparing and says, "Now, the second value is a list of **more_citrus_fruits**. It has an **Orange, Grapefruit, Lemon, Pomelo,** and **Lime**. So far, so good—both lists have the same objects, but let's check the order. Oh! **citrus_fruits** has a **Lemon** at index 1, but **more_citrus_fruits** has a **Grapefruit** instead. Since these two lists don't have the same order, they aren't really equal in my eyes. Time to tell Human that this is **False**."

Now that you know that lists must have the same objects *and* the same order to be truly equal, can you create another list that would return **True** if we compared them?

LISTS CAN BE ACCESSED WITH AN INDEX

When we work with lists in our code, we often deal with a single object from a list at a time. This means that we need an easy way to choose one object from a list, no matter what position it is in. And luckily, there *is* an easy way! *Indices* (the plural of index) give us this ability. An *index* is a number that represents the position of an object within a list. Basically, it tells us where an object is in a list.

Object/Value	'Orange'	'Lemon'	'Grapefruit'	'Pomelo'	'Lime'
Index	0	1	2	3	4

STRINGS AND OTHER THINGS

To use an index, we write code to tell the computer *which list we want to access* and *what position* in the list is holding the object we want. For our **citrus_fruits** list, an example would look like this:

`citrus_fruits[2]`

This code tells the computer to grab the object that's stored at the second index in the **citrus_fruits** list.

Notice how I didn't say that we are grabbing "the second *object*" from the list; instead, I said we are grabbing the object that is "stored at the second *index*" in the list. There is a big difference! Why? Because there is one very important thing to know about lists: their order starts at 0, **not** 1! So, if you tried the previous code, you may have been surprised to get **'Grapefruit'** returned to you instead of **'Lemon'**, like you were probably expecting.

This means the first item in a list would be accessed with the 0 index. Try selecting the first item from the **citrus_fruits** list:

`citrus_fruits[0]`

Did you get an **'Orange'** this time? Sweet!

WHY START AT ZERO?

Even though we count starting from one, computers see order in a different way. When looking at lists, starting at zero means that the first object is quite literally "zero" spaces away from the beginning of the list. This makes sense, as the first item in a list is always the one closest to the opening bracket of a list!

CODING FOR KIDS : PYTHON

LISTS CAN BE SLICED

That may sound painful, but don't worry, it's a normal thing for lists. Just like we slice the piece of pie we want, *slicing* is the method of selecting a specific range of items within a list. It's similar to how we access items in a list with an index, except we can choose more than one item. Instead of placing a single index within the list's brackets, we give it a *slice range*, which includes a starting index, the colon (:) character in the middle, and an ending index. Here's what it looks like:

```
citrus_fruits[2:4]
```

This tells the computer, "Hey there, I need some items from the **citrus_fruits** list. I need all items starting at the second index all the way up to, but not including, the item at the fourth index."

So, this code would result in this output:

```
['Grapefruit', 'Pomelo']
```

Here's what's happening: The first index we give in the **citrus_fruits** list is 2. This is our *starting index*, which is the location of the first item we select in our slice range. We only begin selecting items at this index. The colon (:) character tells the computer we are slicing the list. Once it knows this, it will be looking for an *ending index*, which is the location of the last item in the slice range. This lets the computer know when to stop selecting items. In this case, the ending index is 4. The computer will keep selecting items *until* the ending index, but will not include the item at the ending index itself. This is why **Lime** is not part of this sliced range.

Let's say we wanted the first three items in our **citrus_fruits** array. We can slice it like so:

```
citrus_fruits[:4]
```

which would give us this output:

```
['Orange', 'Lemon', 'Grapefruit', 'Pomelo']
```

You'll notice I didn't give a starting index in this slicing range. This is because the computer assumes you want to start at the beginning of the list if you don't give it a starting index. So, we can write a slice range without the starting index if we know that we need items from the beginning of a list.

This works on the ending index, too. Similarly, to grab only the last three items, we'd write:

```
citrus_fruits[2:]
```

73

which returns this output:

```
['Grapefruit', 'Pomelo', 'Lime']
```

Similar to the starting index, when you don't give the computer an ending index, it assumes you want to select items until the end of the list. So, you can write slice ranges without an ending index if you know that you want items until the end of a list.

LISTS ARE MUTABLE

Once we create a list, we can add new objects, delete existing ones, and move objects around. Being able to change a list in this way means it is *mutable*. The other data types we have learned so far—like strings, integers, and Booleans—cannot change in this way once we've created them. These kinds of data types that cannot change are described as *immutable*.

Earlier, I told you about my favorite desserts. Since lists are mutable, let's change the **my_favorite_desserts** list to store *your* favorite desserts!

For our first change, let's empty out the list by assigning it to an empty list:

```
my_favorite_desserts = []
```

By doing this, we've made a *mutation*, or change, to our **my_favorite_desserts** list. If you look into your list through the shell, it should now be empty:

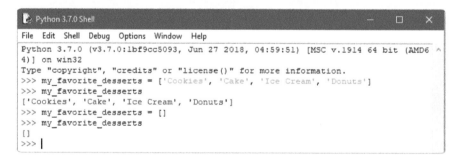

Now, let's make another mutation. Go ahead and add your favorite desserts! (I'll add some different ones here to continue the example, but feel free to add your actual favorite desserts while coding along.)

To do this, we can use something called the *addition assignment operator* (+=) to give our list some new desserts. See how it works:

```
my_favorite_desserts += ['Brownies', 'Muffins', 'Chocolate']
```

Let's check our list again.

```
Python 3.7.0 Shell                                               —    □    ×
File  Edit  Shell  Debug  Options  Window  Help
Python 3.7.0 (v3.7.0:1bf9cc5093, Jun 27 2018, 04:59:51) [MSC v.1914 64 bit (AMD6
4)] on win32
Type "copyright", "credits" or "license()" for more information.
>>> my_favorite_desserts = ['Cookies', 'Cake', 'Ice Cream', 'Donuts']
>>> my_favorite_desserts
['Cookies', 'Cake', 'Ice Cream', 'Donuts']
>>> my_favorite_desserts = []
>>> my_favorite_desserts
[]
>>> my_favorite_desserts += ['Brownies', 'Muffins', 'Chocolate']
>>> my_favorite_desserts
['Brownies', 'Muffins', 'Chocolate']
>>>
```

Great! Our original list has mutated again! This time, it went from being empty to having three new desserts in it. Mutable lists allow us to make tasty changes.

MEMBERSHIP OPERATORS

A common thing we do with lists is check to see if something is or is not within it. We have a special set of operators that do this for us called *membership operators*. These operators go through some input we give them, and will tell us if something we are looking for is or is not in the input.

in

If we wanted to check that a specific item was within a list, we'd use the *in operator*. This looks for a positive confirmation that something exists. So, if we wanted to make sure that Pomelo was in our **citrus_fruits** list, we'd write:

```
'Pomelo' in citrus_fruits
```

continued on next page >>

STRINGS AND OTHER THINGS

and this would be **True**:

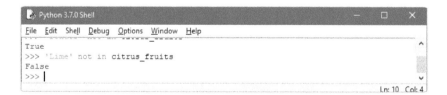

not in

Alternatively, if we want to make sure some item is not in our input, we use the *not in operator*. This looks for a confirmation that something does not exist. Let's say we wanted to make sure that no desserts were in our `citrus_fruits` list. We'd use the **not in** operator like this:

```
'Donuts' not in citrus_fruits
```

Here, we also get **True**, which is correct, as there are no **'Donuts'** in our list:

If we were to check for a **'Lime'**:

```
'Lime' not in citrus_fruits
```

our computer would return **False**, as there *is* a **'Lime'** in our list:

These operators will be very useful in later chapters when we need to filter through lots of data in a collection of items!

MAKING MORE CHANGES TO LISTS

You've already used one method to add to a list, which is the addition assignment operator (+=). There are quite a few more methods, including methods that Python already has built in, for you to make changes to lists. Let's see what they are!

append()

Another way to add an item to a list is to use the built-in *append()* function. This adds an item to the end of the list. Let's say you forgot to add another dessert to your **my_favorite_desserts** list. You can add it quickly, like so:

```
my_favorite_desserts.append('Creme Brulee')
```

Which would result in:

```
['Brownies', 'Muffins', 'Chocolate', 'Creme Brulee']
```

Since we're on a roll, let's add one more dessert!

```
my_favorite_desserts.append('Apple Pie')
```

Our new list is now:

```
['Brownies', 'Muffins', 'Chocolate', 'Creme Brulee', 'Apple Pie']
```

remove()

If we ever need to delete an item from a list, one method we can use is the built-in *remove()* function.

As we take another look at our **my_favorite_desserts** list, we realize that maybe muffins aren't as great as we initially thought, and that we should really delete them from our list. We can use the **remove()** function to do that:

```
my_favorite_desserts.remove('Muffins')
```

After this code, our list would be:

```
['Brownies', 'Chocolate', 'Creme Brulee', 'Apple Pie']
```

STRINGS AND OTHER THINGS

del

Another way we can remove items from the list is using the del keyword. As you can guess, **del** is short for delete. We use this method of deleting an item together with list indices. So, if we needed to remove the item at the first index, we'd write:

```
del my_favorite_desserts[1]
```

And since Chocolate is the item at the first index, that's the item that is deleted. So our resulting list would be:

```
['Brownies', 'Creme Brulee', 'Apple Pie']
```

Keep in mind that slice ranges work, too! So, we could write something like this:

```
del my_favorite_desserts[1:]
```

That would remove **'Creme Brulee'** and **'Apple Pie'** from our list. But why would we want to do that? In case you deleted them by mistake, you can use either the **append()** function or the addition assignment operator (+=) to add them back!

Changes Using Indices and Slice Ranges

Just like we use indices and slice ranges to select one or more items in a list, we can use them to make changes to our list, as well!

For example, if we want to add **'Pumpkin Pie'** as the second item in our **my_favorite_desserts** list, we can do so like this:

```
my_favorite_desserts[1:1] = ['Pumpkin Pie']
```

We write code in this way because there is already an item at the first index. Otherwise, the computer will get confused and do what it thinks you're asking it to do. For example, this won't work the way you think it would:

```
my_favorite_desserts[1] = 'Pumpkin Pie'
```

This will replace the item that's already at that index (in this case, the **'Creme Brulee'**) and put **'Pumpkin Pie'** there instead. That's why you have to be careful when inserting new items at indices that already have items in them. We use the slice range of the same starting and ending index to tell the computer to simply add a new item at that index, without changing the rest of the items in the list. After inserting a new item correctly, our list now looks like this:

```
['Brownies', 'Pumpkin Pie', 'Creme Brulee', 'Apple Pie']
```

Keep in mind that if you are inserting new items into an existing list using this slice range method, it doesn't matter how many items you are adding. So, if we wanted to add Chocolate Souffle, Crepe Cake, and Affogato (gelato drowned in espresso) to our **my_favorite_desserts** list after **'Creme Brulee'**, we'd do this:

```
my_favorite_desserts[2:2] = ['Chocolate Souffle', 'Crepe Cake',
'Affogato']
```

This would make our **my_favorite_desserts** list like so:

```
['Brownies', 'Pumpkin Pie', 'Creme Brulee', 'Chocolate Souffle',
'Crepe Cake', 'Affogato', 'Apple Pie']
```

Pretty neat … and delicious!

TUPLES

Tuples (I like to pronounce them like this: "too-pells," but others pronounce it like this: "tuh-pells"—you decide!) are another type in Python that hold a collection of items or objects. They are very similar to lists, and everything you know about lists is most likely the same for tuples! This means they are ordered, can be accessed with indices, work with slice ranges, and can be made of the same or different types of items. However, there are two major differences between tuples and lists:

TUPLES USE PARENTHESES

Tuples use parentheses ( ) to hold their items, instead of the brackets [ ] used with lists. This means they are created like this:

```
rgb_colors = ('red', 'green', 'blue')
```

But the most important difference of all is that tuples are immutable.

TUPLES ARE IMMUTABLE

Remember, immutable means unable to change. This is a very important difference tuples have from lists. Adding, removing, or changing the contents of tuples is not possible, since this is a special characteristic of tuples! So, this means methods like the **append()** and **remove()** functions and **del** will not work with tuples.

WHEN TO USE TUPLES OVER LISTS

You're probably wondering: *When should I use a tuple and when should I use a list?* That's a great question! For the most part, lists will probably be the type to choose when dealing with collections of items. A big sign that should nudge you to use a tuple is that the collection of items you will be storing shouldn't be changed. Our earlier tuple is a great example of this, as the RGB colors can't change and never should!

IF STATEMENTS

For just a moment, try to think of all the decisions you make in a single day. Even if you narrow it down to just the morning, there are already so many things to decide: Do you wake up when your alarm rings or hit the snooze button one more time? When you finally get up, what outfit do you choose to wear? What do you eat for breakfast? Or do you skip breakfast because you're already running late?

Though it may seem like a hassle, our lives are much more flexible and interesting because we can make so many decisions. Not surprisingly, decision-making also makes our Python programs more flexible and interesting—and therefore smarter.

Just as we make decisions in life, we can make decisions in code by using *if statements*. An **if** statement is a block of code that allows you to control the path the computer will take when it executes your code. This is important because when we write more complex and longer programs, we don't really want the computer to run all of our code. We only want to run certain parts of our code when it makes sense, or when we decide it's the right time to do so. **if** statements give us this decision-making ability. How? They allow us to set up a condition that needs to be met before any additional code is executed. This condition is usually a *Boolean expression*, which

is a condition that the computer evaluates and decides is either **True** or **False**. You can think of Boolean expressions as "Yes or No" questions, where a "Yes" is **True** and a "No" is **False**. When your **if** statement's Boolean expression is **True**, it tells the computer that it should keep going on to the next line of code. The next line of related code is usually right after the **if** statement and is indented. *Indentation* is the amount of space that comes before certain lines of code to help the computer group the blocks of code that belong together.

Here's how to write an **if** statement:

```python
if mood == 'tired':

    hit_snooze_button = True
    print("Adrienne is tired. She hits the snooze button.")
```

Pretty logical, right? If our mood is tired, we will probably choose to hit the snooze button.

Here's what's happening: In this scenario, the Boolean expression we are determining is our **mood**. When the computer gets to that line of code, it asks itself the question, "Is the **mood** equal to **'tired'**?" It either answers, "Yes, the **mood** is definitely equal to **'tired'**, which means this Boolean expression is **True**. This means I can keep going to the next line of code," or it says, "No, the **mood** is not equal to **'tired'**, which means this Boolean expression is **False**. That means I can't keep going onto the next line of code. I'll have to skip to the next line of code I see that has the same indentation as this line." This is important to remember, as the computer will *only* keep going to the next line of code after the colon (:) if it can answer "Yes" to the question (or condition) you give it. If it can't, it skips that code and finds the next line that isn't indented.

start if statement   Boolean expression (Yes/No question)   if True, step into next line of code:

```python
if mood == 'tired':
    hit_snooze_button = True
```

action to do if condition is True

What if we aren't tired, though? What if we want to get up right away because we had a good night's sleep? We can add that decision into our code, too, using an *else if statement*, which is shortened to *elif*.

The code would look like this:

```python
if mood == 'tired':

    hit_snooze_button = True
    print("Adrienne is tired. She hits the snooze button.")

elif mood == 'well-rested':

    get_out_of_bed = True
    print("Adrienne is well-rested. She's already out of bed!")
```

81

Here, we added an elif statement to our code. Always used after a regular **if** statement, an **elif** statement allows you to make a different decision if a different condition is met! It's like asking a different question if the first one you asked was answered with a "No." Using an **elif** statement is perfect for our example, since we are checking for a different condition (`mood == 'rested'`), and are doing something completely different if that condition is **True** (getting out of bed instead of hitting the snooze button).

It's also important to remember that the code after our **if** statement is indented. Indentation is very important in Python, as the computer uses these spaces to figure out which blocks of code belong together. When you want to indent your code, move your cursor to the beginning of the line that you want to indent and simply press the Tab key on your keyboard. This will add the space you need in front of your code. Most of the time, the computer will indent automatically for you, but there will be times you will need to do this yourself.

After adding our **elif** statement, keep in mind that we will only hit the snooze button or we will only get out of bed. We will never do both!

Here's why: When the computer checks our Boolean expressions, it will keep checking each one in our code until it finds one that is **True**. Once it does, it will move to the next line of code that is indented, run all other lines of code that have the same indentation, and then ignore the rest of the Boolean expressions.

In our example, the computer will be able to answer "Yes" when determining if our mood is tired or not. Since it answered "Yes," it moves onto the next line of code that sets the **hit_snooze_button** variable to **True**. It will also print out our message (**"Adrienne is tired. She hits the snooze button."**), since that line of code is also indented like the one before. Since those are the only two lines of code that belong to that indentation group, and seeing that the next line of code is not indented in the same way, the computer will know that it is finished with the **if** statement.

This also means that the computer won't try to evaluate the other Boolean expressions. It ignores the rest because, once it finds a Boolean expression that is **True**, it is almost certain that the other Boolean expressions in the **if** statement would be **False**. (It's *almost certain* because we could have a bug or some incorrect logic written in our code.)

This makes total sense! We can't be "tired" and "rested" at the same time! If we asked the computer "Is our mood tired?", it can't answer both "Yes" and "No"! This is why the computer safely ignores all other Boolean expressions in an **if** statement the moment it finds one that is **True**.

CODING FOR KIDS : PYTHON

DEALING WITH ERRORS AND EXCEPTIONS

As you learn to code, you will deal with many different types of errors and exceptions. This is completely normal! Knowing what kinds of errors and exceptions you'll come across is very helpful, though, so let's go through some of the main types:

Syntax Errors

We've seen this type of error in an earlier chapter. This error means that some part of your code cannot be understood or translated by the computer. Usually, it's caused by an extra character in the wrong spot, a blank space, or a wrong character that is not part of the Python language. When you get these types of errors, keep an eye out for these common bugs and be sure to check your shell! It will usually tell you where the bug is happening.

Type Errors

Type errors are data type problems in code. These can happen when you use a data type that the computer is not expecting or if you try to use a data type in a way that is not allowed by that data type. For example, if you have some code that needs integers as your parameters and you pass strings as your input, you will probably get a type error.

Exceptions

Exceptions are issues with your code that are only found when you run your program. This means that your code can be translated by the computer with no problem, but when it actually performs the actions in your code, the actions themselves cannot be done or cause an issue in another part of your code. A very common exception is one called a *zero division error* (`ZeroDivisionError`). This exception happens when a part of your code tries to divide by zero. The original code you write may not have any code that clearly divides by zero, but you could have a calculation that happens whose result is zero. If that calculation is then used somewhere else, like in another division calculation, it may then cause a zero division error, even though you didn't mean for it to!

As an example, let's say you have some code that takes cookies and divides them by the number of kids available. You expect these two variables to be used like so:

```
def divideCookiesEqually(cookies, kids):
    return cookies / kids
```

But what if you passed into your code 10 cookies and 0 kids? When your code finally executes like this:

```
divideCookiesEqually(10, 0)
```

it tries to do this:

```
10 / 0
```

which would then cause a *division by zero* error (**ZeroDivisionError**)! Don't be afraid or disappointed if you run into these or other kinds of errors. It's part of coding, and it can actually help you think about how to solve many different kinds of problems. It will really stretch your brain! If you ever feel stuck or frustrated, take a break, walk away from the computer, and do something else. Then, come back with a fresh mind and maybe a snack. You will probably see what the error is when you return, or at least you'll have the patience to keep investigating!

CODE COMPLETE!

Phew! We learned a lot more about **strings** in this chapter, and how they work with some of the operators we learned about in chapter 2.

- Strings can be added together to create new strings.

- Strings cannot be added to numeric data types.

- Strings, however, can be multiplied.

We were also introduced to our first mutable (changeable) data type, which is the **list**.

- Lists are a collection of items of the same data type or a mix.

- Lists use **brackets [ ]** to hold their items.

- Lists are ordered and start at 0.

- You can grab specific objects within a list using an **index**.

- You can change lists by adding, reordering, and deleting objects within them.

We learned about **tuples**, which are an immutable (unchangeable) data type similar to lists.

- Tuples can be used in many of the same ways as lists.

- Tuples use parentheses ( ) to hold their items instead of brackets [ ].

- Tuples are not changeable, which is their most important distinction.

- Tuples should be used when the collection of items they hold shouldn't change.

Finally, we also learned how to control the path of our code through **if statements**.

- If statements allow us to make decisions in code.

- Indentation is important and helps us group lines of code that belong together.

- If statements let us tell the computer which parts of our code to run and how.

- If statements use Boolean expressions to figure out what path to take in our code.

In the next chapter, we'll learn about loops! Loops are very useful when it comes to repeating blocks of code or going through larger sets of input data. See you there!

CHAPTER 4 ☆ ACTIVITIES

- -

ACTIVITY 1: THESE ARE A FEW OF MY FAVORITE THINGS

Now that you know how to create lists, try creating one with five of your favorite things! Remember, lists can have a mix of objects in them.

What to Do

Create a list named **my_favorite_things** and add five things to it. Print out a message that says "These are {your name}'s favorite things: ['your', 'favorite', 'things']. Use an f-string to print out this message with your name and your list of favorite things!

Sample Expected Output

```
'These are Adrienne's favorite things: ['Blue', 3, 'Desserts',
'Running', 33.3].'
```

ACTIVITY 2: SHAPESHIFTERS

One day, you and your friend decide to go to the park and watch the clouds. You want to keep track of the different clouds you see and what shapes they look like to each of you, so you both create empty lists (in brackets []) before you begin:

```
your_cloud_shapes = []
friend_cloud_shapes = []
```

While watching, you continue to add the shapes of clouds you see to your lists. Once you go home, you take a look at each other's lists:

```
your_cloud_shapes = ['circle', 'turtle', 'dolphin', 'truck', 'apple', 'spoon']

friend_cloud_shapes = ['apple', 'turtle', 'spoon', 'truck', 'circle', 'dolphin']
```

Interesting! Both of you mostly have the same shapes, but probably saw them at different times!

What to Do

Using **if** statements, the **==** operator, and indices, write some code to check if your cloud shape matches your friend's cloud shape at the same position in each of your lists. You can do this by comparing your object with your friend's object at each index. If your shapes match at the same position, print out "We saw the same shape!" If they don't match, print out "We saw different shapes this time." Go one by one, and compare each item in your list.

Helpful Hints

Remember, you can access specific items in lists by using the indices! Example:
your_list[2]

What to Do

Using your knowledge of string concatenation and accessing list items by index, use the following list of **random_items** to create a proper answer to each scenario that follows. Use f-strings to print the result of your code.

```
random_items = ['basket', 'tennis', 'bread', 'table', 'ball',
'game', 'box']
```

Example
Marie is playing ping-pong with her friends. Another friend, Pierre, says that ping-pong is called something different in his country. Can you form the other name for ping-pong using the **random_items** list?

```
print(f"{random_items[3]} {random_items[1]}")
```

Example Output
```
table tennis
```

Scenario 1
Andre is about to play tennis with some friends. He has his tennis racket, but he needs one more thing. Write some code to print out what he needs!

Scenario 2
Jean just baked some fresh bread. He wants to bring a few loaves home to share. What can you make from the **random_items** list that can help him carry his bread home?

Scenario 3
Christina is singing the words to a popular song that is usually sung at a baseball game. Can you finish the lyrics? "Take me out to the _____ _____!"

Scenario 4
Leslie is writing a story about her favorite sport. It involves a hoop, five players on each team, and a recognizable orange ball with black stripes. Which sport is it?

Scenario 5
Julia just received one of the fresh loaves of bread from Jean. Thanking him, she quickly puts the loaf she received in this item to keep it warm.

Scenario 6
Mario has a lot of board games and video games. Luckily, he can store most of them in this item to keep his room nice and clean!

STRINGS AND OTHER THINGS

ACTIVITY 4: PET PARADE

The local animal shelter is putting on an animal parade for the neighborhood to show off all of the newest animals that need a home! They've asked you to help them organize the order of the pets, based on some different factors.

What to Do

You've learned about the different ways to make changes to lists. Use all of them to help you sort and organize this pet parade! So far, this is the order in which the shelter wants the animals to be shown:

```
pet_parade_order = ['Pete the Pug', 'Sally the Siamese Cat', 'Beau the
Boxer', 'Lulu the Labrador', 'Lily the Lynx', 'Pauline the Parrot',
'Gina the Gerbil', 'Tubby the Tabby Cat']
```

But wait! A good thing has happened! Gina just got adopted, so she no longer needs to be in the pet parade.

Go ahead and remove Gina.

As the planning continues, the animal shelter director decides that Pauline the Parrot should be first in line. Since Pauline can talk, she can start the parade off right by saying hello to the crowd!

Move Pauline to the front of the pet parade order.

Things are moving along, but suddenly, two more animals get dropped off at the shelter (boo). We need to add them to our parade. The first animal is Mimi the Maltese Cat. The second animal is Cory the Corgi. Both of them should go after Lily.

Place Mimi and Cory together so they come after Lily.

Wait a sec, more good news! Lulu and Lily just got adopted by the same owner. He likes both of them very much and thinks they can be good friends.

Remove Lulu and Lily from the pet parade.

That should be it! The pet parade is ready to start. Print out the resulting order of your pet parade after all of the changes we have made.

Expected Output

```
The order of the Pet Parade is: ['Pauline the Parrot', 'Mimi the
Maltese Cat', 'Cory the Corgi', 'Pete the Pug', 'Sally the Siamese
Cat', 'Beau the Boxer', 'Tubby the Tabby Cat'.]
```

ACTIVITY 5: IF THIS, THEN THAT

As we grow older, who we are, what we look like, and what we are interested in will probably change. Let's capture that in an **if** statement and print out what we think we will be like in the next 5, 10, 15, and 20 years.

What to Do

Write an **if** statement that checks for the year, and then output the different predictions you have about yourself for that year! As you can see, I've helped you get started. Write the remaining **elif** statements and make sure to update your variables properly for each year.

Let's capture three things to output with some variables. Create **age**, **favorite_outfit**, and **favorite_hobby** variables, and assign each of them to what they are today.

```
year == 2019
age = 10
favorite_outfit = "red dress"
favorite_hobby = "coding"
```

Next, start your **if** statement and check for the current year:

```
if year == 2019:
```

Then, print out your current description:

```
if year == 2019:
    print(f"It is 2019. I am currently {age} years old, love wearing
    a {favorite_outfit}, and currently, {favorite_hobby} takes up all
    my time!")
```

Now, create four more **elif** statements for 5, 10, 15, and 20 years from now. Adjust your variables, too!

ACTIVITY 6: SLICING AND DICING

Now that you know how to use slice ranges, maybe you can offer some help to Chef Tony. He has crates of fruits and vegetables coming in and needs someone to sort them. If the crate has vegetables, they need to be taken out and moved to the "dicing" area, so his helpers can begin dicing them for the restaurant. If you find fruits, though, they need to be brought to the "slicing" area, so his bakers can prepare the fruits for their desserts.

What to Do

Using slice ranges and the different methods we've learned to add items to a list, write some code for each crate to properly separate the fruits and vegetables and add them to the right area.

I've created two variables for you to start:

```
slicing_area = []
dicing_area = []
```

Once you've gone through all of the crates, print out all of the separated fruits and vegetables.

Here are the crates:

```
crate_1 = ['onions', 'peppers', 'mushrooms', 'apples', 'peaches']
crate_2 = ['lemons', 'limes', 'broccoli', 'cauliflower', 'tangerines']
crate_3 = ['squash', 'potatoes', 'cherries', 'cucumbers', 'carrots']
```

ACTIVITY 7: TO CHANGE OR NOT TO CHANGE

Now that you know the difference between lists and tuples, you can create one or the other for the following collections of items.

What to Do

For each collection of items, create either a tuple or list and store those items within it. Then, print out the contents of the list and which type it is stored in.

Collection 1:

```
first_name, last_name, eye_color, hair_color, number_of_fingers,
number_of_toes
```
Collection 1 Data: **"Adrienne", "Tacke", "brown", "black", 10, 10**

Collection 2: favorite animals
Collection 2 Data: **"cats", "dogs", "turtles", "bunnies"**

Collection 3: colors of the rainbow
Collection 3 Data:
`"red", "orange", "yellow", "green", "blue", "indigo", "violet"`

Sample Expected Output

`('red', 'green', 'blue') are stored in a tuple!`

CHAPTER 4 ☆ CHALLENGES

CHALLENGE 1: CHOOSE YOUR ADVENTURE

Now that we can make decisions with our code using **if** statements, let's create a short Choose Your Adventure story! This game allows you to pick and choose what to do while you go through the story, resulting in a different ending for different decisions! To help you get started, follow these instructions:

1. First, create a Python file called choose-your-adventure and save it.

2. Use the following code to start defining your game:

```python
# Change to your name so you can have your own game!
name = "Your name here"

# Adventure begins.
print(f"Welcome to {name}'s Choose Your Own Adventure game! As you
follow the story, you will be presented with choices that decide your
fate. Take care and choose wisely! Let's begin.")

print("You find yourself in a dark room with 2 doors. The first door
is red, the second is white!")

# This input function allows you to type in your choice. By assigning
it to a variable, you can use the choice that has been made to decide
on the next

# part of the story!
door_choice = input("Which door do you want to choose? red=red door or
white=white door")
```

```python
if door_choice == "red":
    print("Great, you walk through the red door and are now in the
    future! You meet a scientist who gives you a mission of helping him
    save the world!")

    choice_one = input("What do you want to do? 1=Accept or 2=Decline")
    if choice_one=="1":
        print("""_____SUCCESS_____
        You helped the scientist save the world! In gratitude, the
        scientist builds a time machine and sends you home!""")
    else:
        print("""_____GAME OVER_____
        Too bad! You declined the scientist's offer and now you are
        stuck in the future!""")

else:

    print("Great, you walked through the white door and now you are in
    the past! You meet a princess who asks you to go on a quest.")

    quest_choice = input("Do you want to accept her offer and go on the
    quest, or do you want to stay where you are? 1=Accept and go on
    quest or 2=Stay")

    if quest_choice=="1":
        print("The princess thanks you for accepting her offer. You
        begin the quest.")
     else:
        print("""_____GAME OVER_____
        Well, I guess your story ends here!""")
```

Use what you've learned about **if** statements, along with your knowledge of variables, the **print()** function, and several data types to continue this story. Change the outcomes, have more than one decision to make, or set your story in a different setting. It's up to you! Once you are finished, save your game and then run it. You or a friend can now choose your own adventure, and it will be the game *you* created!

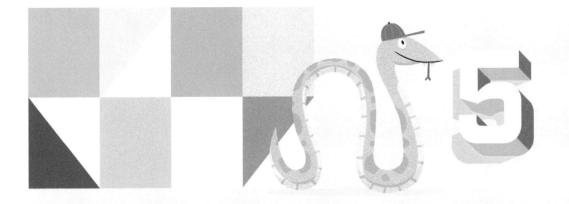

LOOKING AT LOOPS

A big part of why computers are so powerful is that they can repeat many actions or calculations very quickly. One of the ways we can tell a computer to do this is through loops. A loop is a special kind of programming statement that allows you to repeat a block of code. Like all programming languages, Python has two kinds of main loops: for loops and while loops.

FOR LOOP

The first kind of loop is called a *for loop*. This kind of loop repeats a block of code a specific number of times. We usually use **for** loops with lists and when we know how many times we need to repeat a block of code.

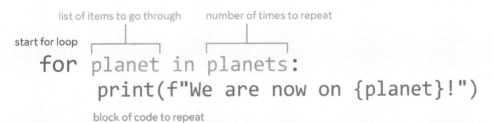

Let's say we create a list of numbers. Let's also say that we want to add 2 to each number in this list and then print the new numbers out. How do we do that? With a **for** loop!

First, let's declare our **numbers** list. We do this because loops always need a group of items to go through. This process of going through a group of items is also called *iterating* through a loop. *Iteration* means going through a group of things one by one.

Let's also fill the **numbers** list with some . . . well . . . numbers!

```
numbers = [1, 2, 3, 4, 5]
```

Awesome! Now, let's begin coding a **for** loop by using the **for** keyword. This keyword signals to the computer that we want to do a **for** loop:

```
numbers = [1, 2, 3, 4, 5]
for
```

Great! Now the computer knows you want to do a loop, but it's like, "Hey Human, it's cool you want me to do a loop and all, but what do you want me to loop through?" We're getting there, machine! Next, let's tell the computer which group of items to go through and how many times to do it. In our case, we want to go through every number in our **numbers** list, so we write the loop to do that:

```
numbers = [1, 2, 3, 4, 5]
for number in numbers:
```

The code we just wrote is the same as telling the computer, *for* every *number in* the **numbers** list, do something. Cool. Now the computer knows which group of items to iterate through. Finally, let's tell the computer to iterate through each number in our list, add 2 to it (because that's the cool thing to do), and print that new number to the console. Remember, the block of code that comes after a colon (**:**) means it belongs to the related line of code above it and should always be indented:

```
numbers = [1, 2, 3, 4, 5]
for number in numbers:
    print(number + 2)
```

And that's it! If you run this code, you should see the results of your **for** loop in your shell.

CODING FOR KIDS : PYTHON

```
Python 3.7.0 Shell                                              —   □   ×

File  Edit  Shell  Debug  Options  Window  Help
Python 3.7.0 (v3.7.0:1bf9cc5093, Jun 27 2018, 04:59:51) [MSC v.1914 64 bit (AMD6 ^
4)] on win32
Type "copyright", "credits" or "license()" for more information.
>>> numbers = [1, 2, 3, 4, 5]
>>> for number in numbers:
        print(number + 2)


3
4
5
6
7
>>>
```

ITERATING THROUGH FOR LOOPS

As we've learned, **for** loops iterate a specific amount of times. The computer knows how many times to iterate based on the *iterator* we give it. In our earlier example, we iterated through every item in the list we passed to our **for** loop:

    for number in numbers:

This works great if we want to go through every item in a list or tuple. But what if we don't want to go through every item? What if we only want to iterate, say, 3 times? Or only go through a specific range of numbers? We can do all of these things!

Every **for** loop requires an iterator and a group of items. When you look at the code for a **for** loop, you can think of it like this:

    for <iterator> in <group of items>:

The `<iterator>` and `<group of items>` are the parts you replace when you create your own **for** loop. So, if we wanted to simply iterate 3 times, rather than iterate through an entire list or tuple with items in it, we would replace the `<iterator>` and `<group of items>` with the following:

    for i in range(3):

Our `<iterator>` is now a new variable **i**, which is the standard name for an iterator variable in programming, and our `<group of items>` is now a range of numbers, which is provided to us by the built-in **range()** function. This function can take up to three parameters (we'll see how to use each of them shortly).

So, this code tells the computer, *for* every *iteration* in the *range of numbers 0–3*, do something. If we add a **print()** function to see how the iterator variable changes, you'll see how this range works:

```
for i in range(3):
    print(i)
```

This results in this output:

```
0
1
2
```

This example shows the **range()** function taking a single parameter, which is a stopping point. However, it can also take another parameter that is a starting point. This allows us to do something similar to slicing in lists and tuples by iterating over a specific range of numbers. So, if we wanted to skip straight to the number 10 and then iterate through the numbers 10 to 20, we'd use the **range()** function like this, using two parameters:

```
for i in range(10, 21):
    print(i)
```

which results in this output:

```
10
11
12
13
14
15
16
17
18
19
20
```

Okay, there's another cool thing we can do with the **range()** function. When we give the **range()** function all three parameters, the third one is used as the *step*, or the number of items to skip when iterating. So, if we only wanted to print the multiples of 10 in the numbers between 0 and 100, we'd use the **range()** function like so:

```
for i in range(0, 101, 10):
    print(i)
```

which results in this output:

```
0
10
20
30
40
50
60
70
80
90
100
```

Pretty neat and very useful!

WHILE LOOP

The second type of loop is a *while loop*. This kind of loop also repeats a block of code over and over, but it will keep repeating as long as a Boolean expression continues to be **True** to the computer. We also use this type of loop with groups of items just like in **for** loops. However, the **while** loop is very different than a **for** loop, because we tend to use the **while** loop when we *don't know* how many times we need to repeat a block of code. Remember that in **for** loops, we know exactly the number of times a block of code needs to be repeated.

Let's say that our **numbers** list from the previous section suddenly contained a lot more numbers:

```
numbers = [1,2,3,4,5,6,7,8,9,10,11,12,13,14,15,16,17,18,19,20]
```

97

Now, instead of adding 2 to every number in the list and printing all of them out to our shell, we decide to go through the list and only print specific ones. To be exact, we only want to print the numbers that, with an addition of 2, become a new number that is less than 20.

How can we do this? Should we use a **for** loop?

Probably not. We don't know beforehand exactly how many times we'll be repeating the code that adds 2. So for this kind of problem, we'll use a **while** loop!

Let's begin by declaring our **numbers** list:

```
numbers = [1,2,3,4,5,6,7,8,9,10,11,12,13,14,15,16,17,18,19,20]
```

Let's also declare our *iterator*, the variable that's used to keep track of the number of loops we run. In programming, we sometimes call this a counter variable because it counts the number of iterations we go through. It is usually named **i**:

```
numbers = [1,2,3,4,5,6,7,8,9,10,11,12,13,14,15,16,17,18,19,20]
i = 0
```

This variable is important. Can you guess why? Keep in mind the differences between **for** loops and **while** loops . . .

Have a guess? Or no clue? It's okay, either way.

Here's why it's important. If you remember what makes **for** loops different from **while** loops, it's that we tell a **for** loop exactly how many times to repeat itself. With **while** loops, we need to give them a little help. That's why we created this iterator variable. When used with our Boolean expression, it acts as a signal to the **while** loop to keep going because we haven't stated exactly how many times to repeat its code. Make sense?

Now, let's start our **while** loop:

```
numbers = [1,2,3,4,5,6,7,8,9,10,11,12,13,14,15,16,17,18,19,20]
i = 0
while
```

Great! Now let's give our **while** loop a Boolean expression to check against. This rule helps the computer decide if it should continue repeating the code or if it should stop. In this scenario, we still want to iterate through all of the numbers in our list. Since we are keeping track of the number of loops we do, we have to use a little bit more logic to tell the computer if we have gone through each object in our **numbers** list. How would we do this?

```
numbers = [1,2,3,4,5,6,7,8,9,10,11,12,13,14,15,16,17,18,19,20]
i = 0
while(i < len(numbers)):
```

That's how! We know that our **numbers** list has a certain number of objects in it. If we iterate through our list the same number of times as the total amount of objects in it, then we know we have gone through them all.

This means our Boolean expression is asking, "Is our iterator variable less than the total amount of objects in our **numbers** list?" If it is, that means we have more numbers to iterate through. And that also means we repeat our loop. Once our iterator is no longer less than the total amount of objects, it means we have iterated through them all, and we can finally stop repeating our loop.

Did you notice that I used a new piece of code in our Boolean expression: **len()**? This is a *function*, which is a reusable block of code that returns a value. This simply means that we receive some sort of output back from the function we use. Usually, the values we receive back are an integer, but they can also be a string, Boolean, list, or any other data type that we might find useful.

The **len()** function isn't just any plain function, though. It is one of Python's many built-in functions! The **len()** function, short for length, takes the input you give it (in this case, our **numbers** list), counts the total number of items in it, and gives that total back to you. That's exactly what we needed for our Boolean expression! We'll learn more about other built-in functions, as well as how to create our own, in the next few chapters.

So, where were we? Ah, now that we have our Boolean expression in place, we can begin writing the code to repeat in our loop. This would be the perfect spot to check and see if the new number we create after adding 2 will be less than 20:

```
numbers = [1,2,3,4,5,6,7,8,9,10,11,12,13,14,15,16,17,18,19,20]
i = 0
while(i < len(numbers)):
    if (numbers[i] + 2) < 20:
```

Keep in mind that we only want to print the number if the Boolean expression in our **if** statement is **True**! That's why we write that code before our actual print statement. Lastly, we indent our **if** statement, since it should only run after it passes the Boolean expression in our **while** loop.

Next, remember how we access specific items in a list? With indices! This time, we'll use them to iterate through each object in our list, and because we have an iterator variable, we can use it to access the next object in the list every time we repeat the loop.

Here's what's happening: Since we know that we will be iterating through all objects in the **numbers** list, and since we started our iterator variable at 0, the first time we enter the loop, our Boolean expression in our **if** statement will be this:

```
if (numbers[0] + 2) < 20:
```

That's exactly what we want as the first time we enter the loop—we want to deal with the first object in the numbers list. Don't forget, lists start at 0!

When we are done with our repeated code, we *increment*, or add, one count to our iterator variable. This means our iterator variable is now set to 1. So, the next loop that repeats means our Boolean expression will now look like this:

```
if (numbers[1] + 2) < 20:
```

Make sense? Because our iterator variable was incremented the last time we ran the loop, and because we are also using the iterator as our index, we are able to get the next item in the **numbers** list! And, just like before, we increment our iterator variable when we are done with our repeated code, so when we repeat the loop the next time, the index we are using also changes. Pretty cool!

CODING FOR KIDS : PYTHON

As we iterate through our loop, we ask the computer the same question: "Hey, if you add 2 to the next number in the numbers list, will the result be less than 20?" If it is, we finally get to the **print()** function and print that number. Again, we indent this code, as it is a new block that only runs after passing the first two levels of Boolean expressions.

```
numbers = [1,2,3,4,5,6,7,8,9,10,11,12,13,14,15,16,17,18,19,20]
i = 0
while(i < len(numbers)):
    if (numbers[i] + 2) < 20:
        print(numbers[i] + 2)
```

Finally, and probably the most important part of **while** loops, we have to add code to increment our iterator variable! Remember, we are the ones keeping track of how many loops we have repeated. We also know how important the **iterator** variable is, because we use it in our **while** loop's Boolean expression and as our index in our **if** statement's Boolean expression:

```
numbers = [1,2,3,4,5,6,7,8,9,10,11,12,13,14,15,16,17,18,19,20]
i = 0
while(i < len(numbers)):
    if (numbers[i] + 2) < 20:
        print(numbers[i] + 2)
    i += 1
```

Notice how I put this code on the same indentation level as the **if** statement? Because there is no other code that needs to be repeated, and because we always want to keep count of how many times we have repeated our loop, we place the increment code (**i += 1**) here right before it starts the loop all over again.

Now, I said this was the most important part of **while** loops. Why? Try running the **while** loop *without* the code to increment our **iterator** variable. What happens?

You've just encountered your first *infinite loop*! Your shell will just keep printing the same number over and over again forever:

On no! To stop it, press and hold the CTRL key then press the C key. Phew, that was wild! An infinite loop is a loop that will repeat itself forever! And we don't want that.

Remember, our **while** loop depends on its Boolean expression to know when to stop. In our example, part of our Boolean expression uses the iterator variable. So, if we never increment our iterator variable, our Boolean expression will always evaluate to the same thing (usually **False**). And if it always evaluates as **False**, then it will never stop the loop! So be careful and try not to create any infinite loops in your code (but at least you know what to do if it happens!).

That's it! If you run this code (with the code to increment the iterator), your results should output something like this:

```
Python 3.7.0 Shell                                        —    □    ✕

File  Edit  Shell  Debug  Options  Window  Help
Python 3.7.0 (v3.7.0:1bf9cc5093, Jun 27 2018, 04:59:51) [MSC v.1914 64 bit (AMD6
4)] on win32
Type "copyright", "credits" or "license()" for more information.
>>> numbers = [1,2,3,4,5,6,7,8,9,10,11,12,13,14,15,16,17,18,19,20]
>>> i = 0
>>> while(i < len(numbers)):
        if (numbers[i] + 2) < 20:
                print(numbers[i] + 2)
        i += 1


3
4
5
6
7
8
9
10
11
12
13
14
15
16
17
18
19
>>> |

                                                          Ln: 28   Col: 4
```

CODE COMPLETE!

In this chapter, we learned about **for** loops and **while** loops. We see how useful they are for repeating blocks of code, and we now know when to use one over the other.

- **For** loops are usually used when we know how many times we need to repeat a block of code.

- **While** loops are usually used when we don't know how many times to repeat a block of code.

- We need to be careful not to write any infinite loops, but there's always CTRL + C to stop it!

- You can create even more complex loops by putting **if** statements within them.

103

Next chapter, we'll take a look at a really cool module that Python has: Turtle! We'll draw shapes, change colors, and move shapes around on the screen. But first, here are some activities to help you hone your loop skills!

CHAPTER 5 ★ ACTIVITIES

ACTIVITY 1: THERE'S A LOOP FOR THAT!

Let's say we wanted to output a greeting to our friends and tell them what our favorite dessert is:

```
print("Hi! My name is Adrienne. My favorite dessert is ice cream.")
```

This works if your name happens to be Adrienne. Oh, and if your favorite dessert also happens to be ice cream. What if it was chocolate? Or cookies? Or cake? What if you had a different name? How would you change the **print()** function to output *your* name and favorite dessert?

You could write a **print()** function for each combination. It would look like this:

```
print("Hi! My name is Adrienne. My favorite dessert is ice cream.")
print("Hi! My name is Mario. My favorite dessert is creme brulee.")
print("Hi! My name is Neo. My favorite dessert is cake.")
```

That's a lot of work, though. If you look at the three **print()** functions, do you notice any kind of pattern? All of them are exactly the same, except for the name and the dessert! This would be a great case to use an f-string and some loops!

What to Do

Write a loop that outputs the name of the person and their favorite dessert using the two lists below. The order of favorite desserts matches the order of the people who like them, so don't worry about that. Use an f-string to print out the message.

```
people = ['Mario', 'Peach', 'Luigi', 'Daisy', 'Toad', 'Yoshi']
desserts = ['Star Pudding', 'Peach Pie', 'Popsicles', 'Honey Cake',
'Cookies', 'Jelly Beans']
```

Expected Result

```
Hi! My name is Mario. My favorite dessert is Star Pudding.
Hi! My name is Peach. My favorite dessert is Peach Pie.
```

. . . (and continued for rest of list)

ACTIVITY 2: LOOP DE LOOP, WHICH HULA HOOP LOOP?

Nacho the cat is walking through the neighborhood, when he sees some hula hoops by a playground. He notices that there are a few placed together by the swings and another group propped up by the basketball court. Nacho gets the idea to invite his friends to come and play.

What to Do

Using your knowledge of loops, write either a **for** loop or **while** loop to cycle through Nacho's cat friends and send them to a specific set of hula hoops.

Nacho has requested for his more athletic or younger friends to be sent to the hula hoops by the swings, since those hula hoops are more difficult to jump through while the swings are in motion. However, if the cat friends are older or less athletic, they should go to the hula hoops propped up by the basketball court, as they are easier to jump through.

Here's some code to help you get started:

```
nachos_friends = ['athletic', 'not athletic', 'older', 'athletic',
'younger', 'athletic', 'not athletic', 'older', 'athletic', 'older',
'athletic']
hula_hoops_by_swings = 0
hula_hoops_by_basketball_court = 0
```

As you cycle through Nacho's friends, determine which group they belong to, then add another count to that group to keep track of how many cats are in each. Finally, print how many cats are at the hula hoops by the swings and how many cats are at the hula hoops by the basketball court.

Sample Expected Output

```
Cats at Hula Hoops by Swings: 6
Cats at Hula Hoops by Basketball Court: 5
```

ACTIVITY 3: IFFY LEGS

Imagine that we worked at a zoo and needed to organize the animals based on the number of legs they have. After organizing them, we also count the total number of animals we have in each group. How would we do this? In real life, we would probably take each animal one by one, look at the number of legs it has, and then put it in an area we've marked as animals having a specific amount of legs. After sorting, we could then count the total number of animals in each area.

Let's try writing a small program to help us sort our animals instead. Sound good?

What to Do

To start, let's create some variables for the different groups of animal legs and assign a starting count of 0 (since we haven't sorted any yet!):

```
has_zero_legs = 0
has_two_legs = 0
has_four_legs = 0
```

Cool! For now, we know that these are the three types of groups that an animal from our zoo can be placed into: a group for animals with no legs, another group for animals with two legs, and a third group for animals that have four legs. Here's some information about the various animals and their number of legs:

```
moose = 4
snake = 0
penguin = 2
lion = 4
```

```
monkey = 2
dolphin = 0
bear = 2
elephant = 4
giraffe = 4
koala = 2
shark = 0
kangaroo = 2
komodo_dragon = 4
```

Create a list with the animal leg information, use a loop to iterate through them all, and keep count of which group we add each animal to. Print out the total number of animals in each group.

Sample Expected Output

```
Animals with no legs: x
Animals with two legs: y
Animals with four legs: z
```

ACTIVITY 4: PASSWORD-PROTECTED SECRET MESSAGE

There are times when we need to share secrets with our friends. Wouldn't it be cool to write a small program that only allows users to see the contents if they provide the right password? Well, we *can* do that using **while** loops!

What to Do

Create a new Python file called secret-message, and save it. In your program, create three variables: one for a password, one for a user's guess, and another for your secret message. I started some below for some inspiration:

```
password = 'cupcakes'
guess = ''
secret_message = 'Tomorrow, I will bring cookies for me and you to
share at lunch!'
```

Now, create a **while** loop. Our **while** loop will be checking the password a person tries through the **guess** variable. Our program should continue to ask for a password if the person's guess is incorrect!

To make sure that only those with the *right* password can view your message, have your **while** loop check to see that your **password** variable is not equal to the **guess** variable. If it isn't, that means the person using your program has not entered the right password or any input at all. In that case, continue the **while** loop and use a **print()** function to ask the user for a password. Also within the **while** loop, keep re-assigning your **guess** variable to whatever the user types into your program like this:

```
guess = input()
```

You should only stop your **while** loop once the user enters the correct password. Once that happens, use another **print()** function to show your secret message!

Save your program, then run it. You should see it continue to ask you for the right password and only show you the secret message once you do!

Sample Expected Output

```
===== RESTART: C:/Users/Adrienne/Documents/Cool Python/secret-message.py =====
What is the password?
hi
What is the password?
hello
What is the password?
password?
What is the password?
i don't know
What is the password?
please
What is the password?
pretty please
What is the password?
you are the best
What is the password?
password
What is the password?
you tell me
What is the password?
cupcakes
Tomorrow, I will bring cookies for me and you at lunch to share!
>>>
```

ACTIVITY 5: GUESS THE NUMBER GAME

Using Python's built-in **random** module (see page 214) and **while** loops, build a simple number guessing game! The computer will pick a random number and assign it to a variable, while you take turns trying to guess that number. Let's code!

CODING FOR KIDS : PYTHON

What to Do

Create a new Python file called guess-the-number-game, and save it. In your program, import the random **module** (by typing **import random** as shown) and create two variables: one to store the number the computer randomly picks, and one for the number of guesses you will allow in your game:

```python
import random

# selects a random number between 1 and 100
number = random.randint(1,100)
number_of_guesses = 0
```

Remember, you can change the range of the random number picked. This is your game!

Now, create a **while** loop that checks your **number_of_guesses** variable to see if it's less than the maximum number of guesses you will allow for your game.

```
<Write some code here>
```

If it is, that means you still have guesses remaining. In that case, continue the **while** loop and write a **print()** function to ask for a number between the range you have selected.

```
<Write some code here>
```

Also within the **while** loop, assign a new **guess** variable to whatever you type into your program, like this:

```python
guess = input()
```

By default, anything you enter into your shell is of the string type. To make sure you can check your number of guesses correctly, transform your **guess** variable into an **int** type by using Python's built-in **int()** function:

```python
guess = int(guess)
```

Now that you've taken another **guess**, you should increase your **number_of_guesses** variable, as well.

```
<Write some code here>
```

Finally, you need to check that the **guess** you've input is equal to the number the computer chose at the beginning of your game. Use an **if** statement for this, and *break* out of (stop) the loop if it is. To do this, simply type the reserved code keyword **break**

`<Write some code here>`

You should only stop your **while** loop once you guess the correct number or if you've run out of chances to guess. In either case, feel free to write a **print()** function that tells you it's game over or that you've correctly guessed the right number!

Save your program, then run it. You should be able to play your secret number guessing game!

Sample Expected Output

```
Python 3.7.0 Shell                                              —   □   ×
File  Edit  Shell  Debug  Options  Window  Help
= RESTART: C:/Users/Adrienne/Documents/Cool Python/guess-the-number-game.py =
Guess a number between 1 and 100:
3
Guess a number between 1 and 100:
97
Guess a number between 1 and 100:
34
Guess a number between 1 and 100:
29
Guess a number between 1 and 100:
33
Guess a number between 1 and 100:
81
Guess a number between 1 and 100:
16
Guess a number between 1 and 100:
93
Guess a number between 1 and 100:
67
Guess a number between 1 and 100:
54
Aww, you ran out of guesses. The magic number was 52.
>>> |
                                                        Ln: 108  Col: 4
```

CODING FOR KIDS : PYTHON

ACTIVITY 6: LOOPING LETTERS

Did you know that you can loop through the letters of a string? You can with **for** loops! Let's loop through our names and count how many vowels are in them.

What to Do

Let's try writing a small program to loop through our names and count how many of each vowel are present. To start, let's create some variables to hold information we'll need:

```
full_name = 'Adrienne Tacke'
number_of_a = 0
number_of_e = 0
number_of_i = 0
number_of_o = 0
number_of_u = 0
```

Now, write a **for** loop to loop through each letter of your **full_name** variable, and if it matches either the letter a, e, i, o, or u, add a count to the proper variable. When you're done iterating through your name, print out the total number of each vowel in your name.

Sample Expected Output

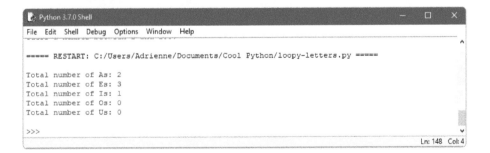

```
Python 3.7.0 Shell                                              —  □  ×

File  Edit  Shell  Debug  Options  Window  Help

===== RESTART: C:/Users/Adrienne/Documents/Cool Python/loopy-letters.py =====

Total number of As: 2
Total number of Es: 3
Total number of Is: 1
Total number of Os: 0
Total number of Us: 0

>>>
                                                              Ln: 148  Col: 4
```

111

CHAPTER 5 ☆ CHALLENGES

CHALLENGE 1: THE CHOCOLATEY COOKIE CHOOSER

Imagine that there is a huge pile of chocolate chip cookies in front of you. Obviously, since you are a chocolate lover, you want to go through the cookies and choose the ones with the most chocolate chips. This means only choosing cookies with *at least 5 chocolate chips* in them. To make sure you get the most chocolatey cookies possible, you also only want the chocolate cookies that were *baked in chocolate batter* (versus the regular batter). Can you write the ultimate chocolate lover function to get the most chocolatey cookies?

The cookie tray is represented by the cookies list declared here:

```
cookies = ['R6', 'C5', 'C3', 'C8', 'R7', 'R7', 'C6', 'C9', 'C10',
'R8', 'C2', 'C7', 'R4']
```

The cookies are labeled as follows: **R** = Regular batter, **C** = Chocolate batter, **n** = number of chocolate chips in the cookie.

Examples:

'R1' means it is a cookie baked in regular batter with only 1 chocolate chip in it (how sad).

'C8' means it is a cookie baked in chocolate batter with 8 chocolate chips in it (bring it on!).

Instructions: Try writing some code that picks the most chocolatey cookies and prints out the list of cookies that match the required rules.

CHALLENGE 2: AN EVEN BETTER GUESS THE NUMBER GAME

The Guess the Number game we created in Activity 5 is pretty fun, but I think we can make it better. Wouldn't it be helpful if the game told you that your guess was too high or too low, so you could make a more educated guess the next time? Also, it would be nice to know how many guesses you have left as you play your game.

What to Do

Open your guess-the-number-game file from Activity 5. Make some changes to your **while** loop so it tells you if your guess is too high or too low when your guess is incorrect. Also, after every incorrect guess, print out how many guesses you have left.

Sample Expected Output

```
Python 3.7.0 Shell
File  Edit  Shell  Debug  Options  Window  Help
>>>
 RESTART: C:/Users/Adrienne/Documents/Cool Python/better-guess-the-number-game.py
Guess a number between 1 and 100:
99
Your guess is too high
Darn, that wasn't the right number. You have 19 chances left to guess the magic number!
Guess a number between 1 and 100:
30
Your guess is too low
Darn, that wasn't the right number. You have 18 chances left to guess the magic number!
Guess a number between 1 and 100:
55
Your guess is too low
Darn, that wasn't the right number. You have 17 chances left to guess the magic number!
Guess a number between 1 and 100:
89
Your guess is too high
Darn, that wasn't the right number. You have 16 chances left to guess the magic number!
Guess a number between 1 and 100:
79
Your guess is too high
Darn, that wasn't the right number. You have 15 chances left to guess the magic number!
Guess a number between 1 and 100:
69
Your guess is too low
Darn, that wasn't the right number. You have 14 chances left to guess the magic number!
Guess a number between 1 and 100:
70
Your guess is too low
Darn, that wasn't the right number. You have 13 chances left to guess the magic number!
Guess a number between 1 and 100:
                                                                          Ln: 120  Col: 0
```

113

LOOKING AT LOOPS

MAY THE TURTLE BE WITH YOU

One of the coolest things about the Python language is that it comes with a lot of prewritten code for you to play with! These groups of ready-made code are called *modules*. The one we'll be diving into for this chapter is the **turtle** module. A module is a Python file that contains code blocks that work with each other and are usually grouped together with other blocks of related code. We'll learn more about them and how to create your own in the next chapter. For now, we'll be using the **turtle** module to create a little turtle, make it move, change its color, and so much more. Let's get started!

USING THE TURTLE MODULE

To start using the **turtle** module, or any other module, we first need to *import* it, which means making the code in the **turtle** module available for us to use. We do this by using the actual word *import* followed by the module we want to use:

```
import turtle
```

Go ahead and import the **turtle** module in your shell as shown (Note: You won't see anything happen yet!).

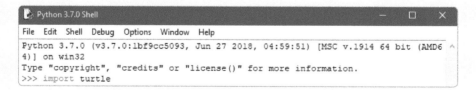

You can think of *importing* as a way to tell the computer to grab a specific instruction manual and have it ready before we continue with the rest of our code. Here, we are saying, "Hey computer, we really want to draw some turtles and play around with them. We know that this kind of code is already written for us in the **turtle** module, so could you grab the code that belongs in that module? That way, when we ask you to do something, you can look up how to do it in the **turtle** module!" Yes, we tell the computer all of that in a single **import** statement!

CREATING A TURTLE

Once you've imported the **turtle** module, you still won't see anything on your screen. Don't worry, this is normal. Behind the scenes, though, we now have access to the different pieces of code the **turtle** module gives us, so that means we can create a turtle! To do this, use the **turtle** module's **shape()** function to tell the computer what kind of shape to draw:

```
turtle.shape('turtle')
```

Go ahead and type that into your shell.

```
Python 3.7.0 Shell                                          —   □   ×
File  Edit  Shell  Debug  Options  Window  Help
Python 3.7.0 (v3.7.0:1bf9cc5093, Jun 27 2018, 04:59:51) [MSC v.1914 64 bit (AMD6
4)] on win32
Type "copyright", "credits" or "license()" for more information.
>>> import turtle
>>> turtle.shape('turtle')
>>> |
```

What happens after you press **ENTER**?

```
Python Turtle Graphics

              🐢
```

Hey! There's our turtle! It's so cute. What will you call yours? I'll call mine Tooga.

You'll see that a separate window has opened where Tooga is just chilling. This is part of the code that's already written for us in the **turtle** module. Whenever you use the **turtle** module, it allows you to play around with two things: a **Screen** object, which is the window that will hold your turtle, and a **turtle** object, which is the little turtle you created. Since the **turtle** module creates these two things, and since it is a ready-made module with all kinds of code already written for us to interact with these objects, we can get really creative!

One last thing—write this code:

```
turtle.setup(500, 500)
```

This will make our window size a little bit smaller so that it's easier to work with and make sure that Tooga doesn't leave a trail behind (we'll talk more about this function in a bit). For now, let's have some fun with Tooga's home (a.k.a. the screen)!

TOOGA'S HOME

Tooga seems to be enjoying his window of a home. We can make it a bit more fun, though! To start, let's change the color of his home. We can do this by using the **Screen** object's **bgcolor()** function. The **bgcolor()** function is a prewritten block of code that changes the background color of the turtle's screen to one that you decide! We use it like this:

```
turtle.Screen().bgcolor("blue")
```

Here's what's happening: First, we need to tell the computer which object we want to interact with. In this case, it's the **Screen**. Because the **Screen** object belongs to the **turtle** module, we make this connection known using dot notation. In modern programming styles, *dot notation* is a way to show that certain blocks of code are related to each other. So, to tell the computer we want to specifically use the **Screen** object that belongs to the **turtle** module, we use a dot (.) in between them. That's how we get the first part:

```
turtle.Screen()
```

But we're not finished yet! We still have to tell the computer to use a specific function that belongs to the **Screen** object to change the color. In our case, it's the **bgcolor()** function. Just as before, we put a dot in between the **Screen** object and the name of the function we want to use:

```
turtle.Screen().bgcolor()
```

Finally, we give the **bgcolor()** function a color:

```
turtle.Screen().bgcolor("blue")
```

So, altogether, the computer understands our code to mean, "Please find the **turtle** module's **Screen** object. When you do, find the **bgcolor()** function that belongs to it. Finally, do what the **bgcolor()** function says to do with the color we've given it." In this case, it's blue. Remember, we didn't write the code for this; it's already written for us in the **turtle** module. That's why we needed to import the **turtle** module first before using it. Now, the computer can go through the **turtle** module's code, find the objects and functions we are asking it to use, and run the code that is already written for us. Neat!

TO HAVE PARENTHESES OR TO NOT HAVE PARENTHESES

Why does **Screen** have parentheses (), but **turtle** does not? If you look back at the code we wrote, you'll see:

```
turtle.Screen().bgcolor("blue")
```

This is part of a modern programming style called *object-oriented programming*. In *object-oriented programming*, programmers focus on writing code that is organized into groups that are related, can be reused, and can work with each other like building blocks. This way, code can be written into modules that we use directly, like the **turtle** module, or written in a way that we have to create a copy of it, like the **Screen** object. In Python's **turtle** module, the **Screen** object is something we have to create a copy, or *instance*, of, because we might want to make changes to it. You'll notice this more and more as you work with other modules and object-oriented languages.

If you've followed along so far, Tooga's home should now be blue. This means that writing this code:

```
Python 3.7.0 Shell

File  Edit  Shell  Debug  Options  Window  Help

Python 3.7.0 (v3.7.0:1bf9cc5093, Jun 27 2018, 04:59:51) [MSC v.1914 64 bit (AMD6
4)] on win32
Type "copyright", "credits" or "license()" for more information.
>>> import turtle
>>> turtle.shape('turtle')
>>> turtle.setup(500, 500)
>>> turtle.penup()
>>> turtle.Screen().bgcolor('blue')
>>> |

                                                                        Ln: 8  Col: 4
```

should result in this home for Tooga:

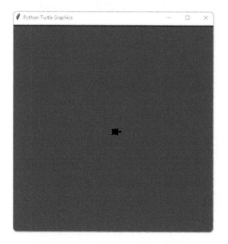

Whoa! That's *really* blue. Also, not the kind of blue I was hoping to give to Tooga's home. I like to think of turtles in the ocean, so I want to choose a nicer and very specific shade of blue that's more like ocean water. Luckily, we can do that! But before we do, let's talk a little bit about how colors work.

COLORS ARE JUST A LITTLE R, G, AND B

On a computer, all colors are really just specific combinations of the three *primary additive colors*, which are red, green, and blue. Computers use *additive* color, which means colors are created by adding different levels of red, green, and blue together. This makes sense, because computer screens give off light and can only combine levels of light to make colors! When choosing colors on a computer, we need to tell it exactly how much of each primary color to use to get the resulting color we want. This is called the *RGB color model*. The RGB color model stands for the red green blue color model

CODING FOR KIDS : PYTHON

and is written using three numbers, with each number representing how much red, green, and blue should be used:

`(R, G, B)`

Each number represents the amount of red, green, and blue contained in the specific color you want. The first number is how strong you want the red color to be. If you wanted the strongest red and absolutely no other color, you'd give the RGB model the maximum amount of red, zero for green, and zero for blue:

`(255, 0, 0)`

Similarly, for the strongest green color, you'd give the maximum amount of green, and no red or blue:

`(0, 255, 0)`

And lastly, to create a total blue, you would have no red and no green:

`(0, 0, 255)`

Why is the maximum amount 255? Let's explore a little deeper! We use this number because of how computers store information. Computers uses the numbers 0 and 1 to process information. A ***bit***, which is short for binary digit, is the smallest unit of data a computer can hold. A bit represents either a 0 or a 1, which literally means "off" or "on." A ***byte*** is another unit of measurement the computer uses to represent information like letters or numbers. One byte is equal to eight ***bits***. It also happens to equal exactly one RGB value! So, in 8-bit binary, this makes the number 0 equal to 00000000 and the number 255 equal to 11111111. As you can see, the most amount of data we can store is the same as using up all eight bits in a single byte. And since an RGB value is exactly one byte of data, this translates to the maximum number of 255 for RGB values. You never know—some of this stuff might help you win on *Jeopardy*!

THE HEXADECIMAL SYSTEM

The color I wanted for Tooga's home is #1DA2D8. Now, you may be wondering what color #1DA2D8 is. It's actually the very specific shade of blue that I wanted to give Tooga's home, written in hexadecimal form. The ***hexadecimal system*** is a number system that uses 16 symbols to represent numbers, which are 0, 1, 2, 3, 4, 5, 6, 7, 8, 9, A, B, C, D, E, and F. Since it has 16 symbols to represent unique numbers, we consider hexadecimal to be a base-16 number system.

continued on next page >>

MAY THE TURTLE BE WITH YOU

We humans are used to a **base-10** system, which we call the decimal system. We use exactly 10 symbols, which you are probably familiar with: 0, 1, 2, 3, 4, 5, 6, 7, 8, and 9. These are the only symbols we use to create all of our numbers.

The hexadecimal system allows the computer to store more information with less code, since it uses 16 different symbols to represent numbers. Just take a look at a sample of what our decimal numbers are when written as hexadecimal numbers:

Decimal (Base 10)	Hexadecimal (Base 16)	Decimal (Base 10)	Hexadecimal (Base 16)
0	0	11	B
1	1	12	C
2	2	13	D
3	3	14	E
4	4	15	F
5	5	16	10
6	6	100	64
7	7	200	C8
8	8	250	FA
9	9	255	FF
10	A		

From the moment we reach 10 in the decimal system, we are already required to use two characters. In hexadecimal, we still only use one character for the number 10, which is "A." This means we are already saving the space of one character.

In this system, the different characters go together to create a 6-digit **hexadecimal color**. The first pair of characters in a hexadecimal color is the R value, the second pair is the G value, and the third pair is the B value. The big difference between this and the decimal system is that we just use 6 characters—"1DA2D8" instead of a possible 9 (if you translate this color, though, it's only eight: 29, 162, 216). To make these numbers a hexadecimal color, we add a # sign in front of the numbers, which tells the computer that it is a hexadecimal number!

CODING FOR KIDS : PYTHON

TOOGA'S HOME 2.0

Back to Tooga . . .

Now that we know how to get specific colors using the RGB model, let's give Tooga the right shade of blue for his home. First, we have to tell the **turtle** module that we want to use the RGB scale of colors, instead of the standard "named" colors. Here's how:

```
turtle.Screen().colormode(255)
```

Nice! Now the computer will know that we will be giving it specific red, green, and blue values! Let's pass them to the **bgcolor()** function next:

```
turtle.Screen().bgcolor(29, 162, 216)
```

Sweet! Tooga should now have an awesome ocean blue setting for his home:

Much better! It's getting a little hard to see little Tooga, though! But, just as we can change the screen's color, we can also change Tooga's!

TOOGA'S TRUE COLORS

Now that we've changed Tooga's home to be a nicer shade of blue, let's make him a nice turtle green! The code is similar to our earlier example, except we are changing the **turtle** object instead of the **Screen** object. Can you guess what the code will look like?

```
turtle.color(9, 185, 13)
```

Exactly! We are changing the **turtle** object itself, so we call our **turtle** object directly. Then, we use the **turtle** module's **color()** function to give it a specific shade of green, using RGB values. Remember, you can always choose your own colors, so feel free to pick a different color for your turtle! Tooga should be a nice green now:

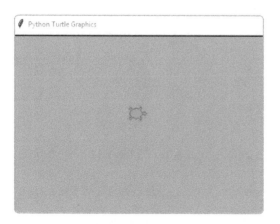

He's green! However, Tooga is still a little hard to see. Let's try adding an outline color to him to help make his turtle shape stand out. We can use the **pencolor** function for this!

```
turtle.pencolor(0, 128, 0)
```

This should now give Tooga a darker green outline:

But even with these color changes, it's still quite hard to see Tooga, so let's make him a little bigger. Yes, we can!

CODING FOR KIDS : PYTHON

BIG TOOGA OR LITTLE TOOGA?

Since Tooga's home is quite large, it can be sort of hard to see him in the middle of all that ocean water. To fix this, let's make him a little bit bigger so it's easier to find him! We can do this by using the **turtlesize()** function:

```
turtle.turtlesize(10, 10, 2)
```

The **turtlesize()** function uses three numbers as its input: The first and second numbers are used to stretch the turtle lengthwise (up and down) and widthwise (left and right) a certain amount. The third number sets the size of the turtle's outline, which is the part of Tooga that is a darker green. As you can see, our code above did make Tooga bigger. Whoa! Maybe a little too big:

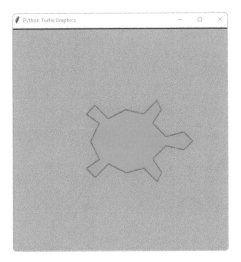

No worries! We can bring him back to original size. If you ever need to reset your turtle to the original size, you can do so by using the **resizemode()** function:

```
turtle.resizemode('auto')
```

This will bring your turtle back to the original size. The **'auto'** parameter just tells the computer to use the default values the **turtle** module originally gave us. Let's try resizing Tooga again, but not as big this time!

```
turtle.turtlesize(3, 3, 2)
```

Ahh, just right! These inputs give me a perfect-sized Tooga. Not too big, but not too small either:

MAY THE TURTLE BE WITH YOU

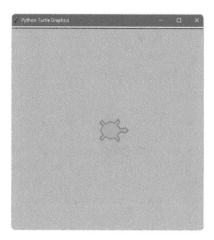

Now, you may be wondering about that third parameter in the **turtlesize()** function—something about the outline? Yes, this number decides how thick or how thin Tooga's outline should be. So, if you give the **turtlesize()** function a third input, it acts as a shortcut to also resize the outline. Of course, you can always change the outline thickness directly, without having to change Tooga's size. To do this, we just give the **turtlesize()** function a single input and what it should be used for:

```
turtle.turtlesize(outline=10)
```

When you do this, Tooga's outline will be a bit thicker!

I think that outline is too thick, so I'm going to change it:

```
turtle.turtlesize(outline=3)
```

This looks much better:

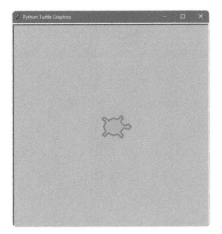

Now that Tooga is the right size and color, let's get him comfortable with his surroundings!

MOVING TOOGA AROUND

Tooga is quite enjoying his home. There's so much water to swim around in! To enjoy it, you can move Tooga around using the **forward()** and **back()** functions. Both functions take a number as an input and will be the number of pixels Tooga will move across the screen. *Pixels*, short for picture element, are the small little dots that make up what we see on a computer screen. They are the most common unit of measurement used when we deal with pictures and drawings! So, to move Tooga forward 200 pixels, you'd write:

`turtle.forward(200)`

Look at that! He's moved to the right!

MAY THE TURTLE BE WITH YOU

And to move him backward 350 pixels, you'd write:

```
turtle.back(350)
```

Now he's moved back toward the left side of the screen!

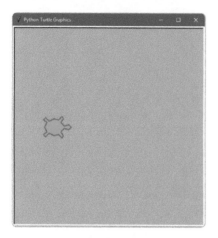

Splish-splash, Tooga's having fun swimming around! He's moved to the right, and he's moved to the left of the screen. Now he wants to explore the top and bottom parts! How do we do that?

Well, how would *you* move toward something that you wanted to go to? You'd probably turn your body in the direction of your target, and then start walking toward it, right? We write the same kind of code to turn Tooga around! Let's say we wanted to move Tooga to the top of the screen. What direction would he first have to turn toward in order to face the top?

Left! So we move Tooga to the left a certain amount:

```
turtle.left(90)
```

Nice. Tooga should now be facing the top of the screen. That's exactly what we want, as that's the direction we're heading!

Here's what's happening: The number of units you pass into the **left()**, and soon, **right()**, function act as *degrees*. Just like in math, these are measurements that determine how far around you've moved in a circle. If you've turned 360 degrees, it means you've turned around in a full circle, and you'd be facing the same direction as when you started. Turning 180 degrees means you would end up facing in the complete opposite direction from where you started. These degree measurements, when passed as numbers to the **left()** and **right()** functions, are very useful in turning Tooga around so he can move in very specific directions!

Now, you know the rest. Move Tooga forward to bring him to the top of the screen:

```
turtle.forward(200)
```

Whee! Tooga has now explored part of the top of his ocean screen home!

All that's left is to explore the bottom of the screen. Think we can get him near the bottom-right corner? Remember, we first need to turn him toward the correct direction, and then we can move him!

One way we could do this is to first turn him way around to the right:

```
turtle.right(150)
```

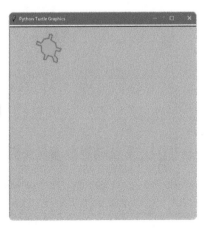

MAY THE TURTLE BE WITH YOU

Then, we can move him forward enough pixels to get him to the bottom right:

`turtle.forward(300)`

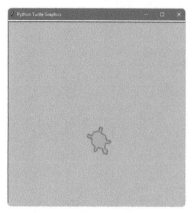

Looks like we're a little short. Let's move him a few more pixels forward to get him closer to the bottom-right corner.

`turtle.forward(200)`

That's a little better! Now Tooga has explored his home! You can keep playing around and let Tooga explore his ocean screen home until you're comfortable with the **forward()**, **back()**, **left()**, and **right()** functions.

DOODLES AND SHAPES

Even though it's called the **turtle** module, we can actually use it for drawing and creating shapes as well. The **turtle** object gives us many functions that can be reused for drawing on the **Screen** object. Let's see how we can do that!

CREATING A PEN

To start drawing, we need a tool to draw with! For that, we can create an instance of the **turtle** object and call it pen.

```
pen = turtle.Turtle()
```

Remember, since an instance is a copy of an object, we get all of the pre-built functions that come with the original object! So, that means our **pen** variable can use the same functions we used earlier. That's how we can write code like this:

```
pen.color("blue")
pen.pensize(5)
pen.forward(100)
```

Do those functions look familiar? That's because they are! We used them with Tooga earlier in this chapter. In Tooga's case, we used these functions to change Tooga and make him move. Now, since we want to use the **turtle** object to draw, we reuse these same functions to help us draw instead of moving an object around!

CREATING A SHAPE

Let's keep using our pen to draw. How would you draw an orange square? Think about how you would draw one in real life with your hand. You'd probably pick an orange-colored pen to start. In code, we'd do the same thing! We would "pick" our color by changing the color of our pen:

```
pen.color("orange")
```

Next, we would move our pen in the shape of a square. This would mean moving our hand to create four equal lines in four different directions until our line ends where we started. How would this look in code? Remember, we can use any of the functions we've already used with Tooga, since we're using the same object to power our pen!

To start, we'd draw the first line. So in code, it could be something like this:

```
pen.forward(100)
```

Which means your screen would look like this:

Now, what direction would you move your pen to continue drawing a square? Probably up, toward the top of the page, right? In code, that's the same as turning the direction of the pen. And we already know how to do that! So, to turn our pen upward, we'd need to turn it to the left about 90 degrees:

```
pen.left(90)
```

Then, we'd draw another line that's the same size:

```
pen.forward(100)
```

Now our square is half complete!

CODING FOR KIDS : PYTHON

All that's left are two more sides to our square. I think you know what to do :)

```
pen.left(90)
pen.forward(100)
pen.left(90)
pen.forward(100)
```

After this code, our square should be complete:

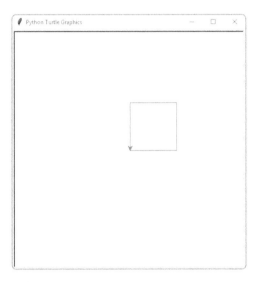

Awesome! You may notice that the arrow shape is kind of blocking our cool new square, though. Luckily, we can hide it so we can see our full square in all its glory. To do that, use the **hideturtle()** function:

```
pen.hideturtle()
```

The **hideturtle()** function does just that: it hides the shape of the **turtle** object you are currently using. Although we are using a copy of the **turtle** module that we just named "pen," the names of the functions that it comes with will still be related to the original **turtle** object. That's why the function is called **hideturtle()** and not hidepen, for example.

Now we should see all of our square:

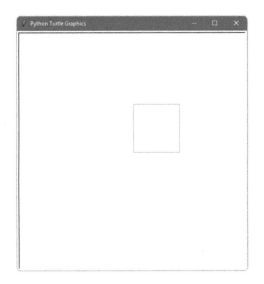

For this shape, we repeated the same code a specific number of times. This means that we can probably make this code even better! What block of code can we use to draw this same square with less repeated code? Did you say a **for** loop? If so, you're right!

```
for i in range(1, 5):
    pen.forward(100)
    pen.left(90)
```

That's much better! Whenever we can make our code easier to understand, as we did here by using less code, it's best to do so. That way, if we ever need to look back at our code, we'll know exactly what's happening.

FILLING SHAPES WITH COLOR

For most of this chapter, we've been drawing shapes that are just outlines. However, that doesn't mean we can't fill them with color! To draw a shape that is filled in, we first have to tell the computer what color we want to fill our shape with:

```
pen.fillcolor('orange')
```

Then we signal to the computer that we want to fill the shape we are about to draw:

```
pen.begin_fill()
```

CODING FOR KIDS : PYTHON

Now, you can begin drawing any shape you'd like. Free draw by giving the pen directions to move it around, or read on and use one of the built-in functions (which we cover right after this section). For this section, I'll choose a circle:

`pen.circle(50)`

And now we will tell the computer that we're finished drawing our shape, so it can finish the color-filling process:

`pen.end_fill()`

Voilà! A nice orange circle:

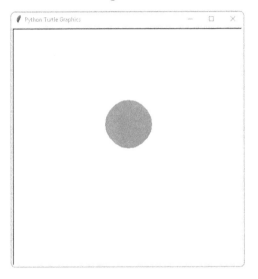

USING BUILT-IN FUNCTIONS

Did you know that the **turtle** object also has some *built-in functions* to create some cool drawings? Let's go over them now!

circle()

The **circle()** function is used to create … you guessed it, circles! The **circle()** function takes up to three parameters, all of which are **int** types:

`circle(radius, extent, steps)`

When you use this function to draw circles, you have to give at least one parameter, which will be used as the *radius* (size) input. So, if we wrote this:

`pen.circle(100)`

we would draw a circle with a radius of 100.

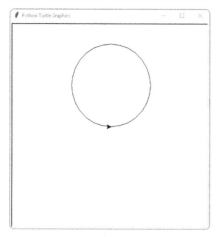

This is the simplest way to draw circles. But what happens if we give the **circle()** function two parameters? Well, the values would fill the radius (size) and extent (distance) parameters. So if we wrote this code:

```
pen.circle(100, 180)
```

we are telling the computer to draw a circle with a radius of 100 (first parameter), but to draw it only to the *extent* of 180 degrees (second parameter). This would result in an exact half of a circle, or *semicircle*, because a full circle is equal to 360 degrees.

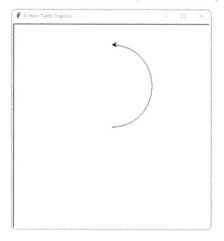

Finally, if we use all three parameters in the **circle()** function, the third parameter steps (direction) would change the direction of the drawing by the value passed into it. So, this code:

```
pen.circle(200, 270, 30)
```

CODING FOR KIDS : PYTHON

tells the computer, "Hi there, can you draw me a circle with a radius of 200, but only to the extent of 270 degrees, and turn the pen by 30 degrees as you are drawing?" That's a complex set of instructions! But it results in something fun.

As you can see, it begins drawing a sort of swirl! There are so many kinds of shapes and doodles you can draw using the **circle()** function. Try changing the parameters around to see what you can create. Don't forget to change the pen color and size to get even more creative with your drawings!

stamp()

Another really cool built-in function the **turtle** object gives us is the **stamp()** function. Just like it sounds, the **stamp()** function "stamps" a copy of the shape you select each time you use it. To see this in action, let's first create a copy of the **turtle** object, set it to the turtle shape, and make it green:

```
turtle_stamp = turtle.Turtle()
turtle_stamp.shape('turtle')
turtle_stamp.color('green')
```

Let's hide the line that is usually drawn when moving the **turtle** object, since we want to see the stamps:

```
turtle_stamp.penup()
```

And now the fun part: To start stamping, simply move your turtle to the next position you want to stamp, and then use the function:

```
turtle_stamp.forward(100)
turtle_stamp.stamp()
```

MAY THE TURTLE BE WITH YOU

Whoa! See how that stamps your turtle shape? Let's create a few more:

```
turtle_stamp.left(90)
turtle_stamp.forward(100)
turtle_stamp.stamp()
turtle_stamp.left(90)
turtle_stamp.forward(100)
turtle_stamp.stamp()
turtle_stamp.left(90)
turtle_stamp.forward(100)
turtle_stamp.stamp()
```

After doing this, you should have four turtle stamps!

Things can get even more interesting when you combine the **stamp()** function with **for** loops! For example, to create a turtle spiral, try this code:

```
import turtle
# make the random module available for us to use
# this one allows us to generate random numbers!

import random

# create a stamp
stamp = turtle.Turtle()

# make it a turtle shape
stamp.shape('turtle')
```

```
# lift the color of the stamp so we don't draw a continuous line
stamp.penup()

# set RGB color mode to allow random colors in RGB
turtle.colormode(255)

# set some variables
# one for the initial distance to move (paces)
# and three more to hold the starting RGB values
paces = 20
random_red = 50
random_green = 50
random_blue = 50

# start a for loop to repeat the stamping code
# repeat 50 times

for i in range(50):
    # use random function to pick a random number for the
    # red value
    random_red = random.randint(0, 255)
    # repeat random function for green
    random_green = random.randint(0, 255)
    # repeat random function for blue
    random_blue = random.randint(0, 255)
    # set the stamp color with the randomly chosen RGB
    # values
    stamp.color(random_red, random_green, random_blue)
    # STAMP! Stamp a turtle with the colors from the last
    # step
    stamp.stamp()
    # add more paces
    paces += 3
    # move forward by the new number of paces
    stamp.forward(paces)
    # slightly turn direction as we move to start spiraling
    stamp.right(25)
```

MAY THE TURTLE BE WITH YOU

Executing this code results in this:

Just like the **circle()** function, the **stamp()** function provides endless possibilities for drawings and even games! Try out different shapes and colors to see what you can create!

write()

Another fun built-in function the **turtle** object provides is the **write()** function. If you ever need to write text on your screen, this is the function to use. It's similar to the **print()** function:

```
pen = turtle.Turtle()
pen.write("Turtles rock!")
```

This will use the current pen size and color for the text. If we want to change the *font*, which is the typestyle, and the size of the text we write, we can give the **write()** function a second parameter! I'm going to change my font to one that's easy to read, change the size, and make it a normal type (instead of **bold** or *italicized*):

```
pen.write("Turtles rock!", font=("Open Sans", 60, "normal"))
```

See what we did there? The first parameter is the text we want to output, and the second parameter is a tuple that holds details about the font! Executing this code, we get this:

Python Turtle Graphics

.Turtles Rock!

Are you getting excited about all the wonderful possibilities this function and other functions can provide you while coding? There's so much you can do!

CODE COMPLETE!

That was fun! We learned about the **turtle** module, a lot of the cool things we can do with it, and even made a new friend—thanks, Tooga!

- Python comes with a **turtle** module, which has a library of ready-to-use functions and code for us to play with.

- The **turtle** module gives us **turtle** and **Screen** objects to use for drawing, creating shapes, and interacting with a screen.

- We learned how to create our little turtle friend.

- We changed the color of the turtle's home (the screen)!

- We changed the turtle's colors, outlines, and size.

- We learned how to move and rotate the turtle around the screen.

While making friends with our little turtle, we also learned some important things about computers.

- We learned what the **RGB color model** is and how it can help us choose specific colors on a computer.

- We learned how information is stored and what **bytes** and **bits** are.

MAY THE TURTLE BE WITH YOU

Finally, we learned how to use the **turtle** module for drawing and creating shapes.

- We created some pens.

- We learned how to change colors and pen sizes.

- We learned how to draw shapes and fill them with color.

- We learned how to stamp.

So many things in one module! Next, we'll learn how to create our own modules and functions.

CHAPTER 6 ★ ACTIVITIES

- -

ACTIVITY 1: LET'S DRAW A STAR!

Now that we've learned about the **turtle** module and what it can do, let's draw a star! We'll create a small program that can do this for us.

What to Do

1. Create a Python file and save it with the name star.

2. Import the **turtle** module:

```
import turtle
```

3. Set the **colormode** to 255:

```
turtle.colormode(255)
```

4. Create a **pen** variable and assign it a **turtle** object. This makes it easier to understand that we're drawing something instead of dealing with a turtle!

```
pen = turtle.Turtle()
```

5. Choose some RGB values for a shade of yellow you like, or choose a different color. For this activity, I'm using a bright yellow:

```
pen.color(255, 215, 0)
```

6. Let's also change the pen size so our star is nice and visible! You can choose whatever size you want:

```
pen.pensize(5)
```

7. Now let's hide the shape so we can see our star a bit better:

```
pen.ht()
```

8. Let's draw! We'll move our pen forward by 100 units, then turn our pen 144 degrees to the right. We'll do this five times to create a five-pointed star. So, the code will look like this:

```
pen.forward(100)
pen.right(144)

pen.forward(100)
pen.right(144)
pen.forward(100)
pen.right(144)
pen.forward(100)
pen.right(144)
pen.right(144)
```

9. Finished! Save your code by pressing the **CTRL** and **S** keys together. Then press the **F5** key to see your star drawn in front of you! Bonus: Can you optimize the code above to use a **for** loop instead?

Sample Expected Output

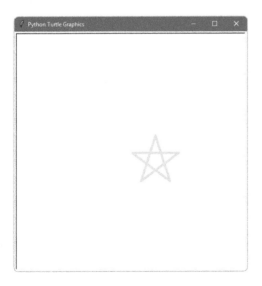

What to Do

Create a new file called fortune-teller, and save it. Within it, import the **Turtle** module and **random** module:

```
import turtle
import random
```

Create a new copy of the **turtle** object, and call it **pointer**; you can leave it as the default arrow shape because that's what we'll need! Also, set its size:

```
pointer = turtle.Turtle()
pointer.turtlesize(3, 3, 2)
```

Create another copy of the **Turtle** object, and call it a **pen**. We'll use this to create our fortune-teller board:

```
pen = turtle.Turtle()
```

Finally, create a variable to hold your spinner amount, and use the **random** module to pick a random number:

```
spin_amount = random.randint(1,360)
```

Now, lift your **pen** so that it doesn't start drawing. We only want it to draw at the spots we tell it to:

```
pen.penup()
```

Use the **goto()** function to move your **pen** to the four sides of your screen. On each side, write some answers that your fortune-teller pointer can land on. These can be simple "Yes" or "No" answers or silly ones like "Never in a million years!" To help you out, I've provided the coordinates for the four sides of the screen:

```
# right side
pen.goto(200, 0)
pen.pendown()
pen.write("Yes!", font=('Open Sans', 30))
pen.penup()

# left side
pen.goto(-400, 0)
pen.pendown()
```

```
pen.write("Absolutely not!", font=('Open Sans', 30))
pen.penup()

# top side
pen.goto(-100, 300)
pen.pendown()
pen.write("Uhh, maybe?", font=('Open Sans', 30))
pen.penup()

# bottom side
pen.goto(0, -200)
pen.pendown()
pen.write("Yes, but after 50 years!", font=('Open Sans', 30))
pen.ht()
```

Finally, pass your **spin_amount** variable into your pointer's **left()** or **right()** function to make it spin a certain direction.

Save your file. Now, every time you run your fortune-teller program, you will get a random answer to your questions!

ACTIVITY 3: RAINBOW TURTLES!

What to Do

Using your knowledge of the **stamp()** function, create a program that stamps a turtle in each color of the rainbow. Make sure the turtles are in the same order as the colors of the rainbow!

Helpful Hints

Use a **for** loop to iterate through the steps you need to repeat. This includes changing the color of the turtle, stamping, and moving the turtle a certain amount.

Sample Expected Output

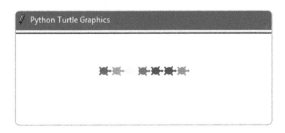

MAY THE TURTLE BE WITH YOU

ACTIVITY 4: CIRCLECEPTION

Create a circle within a circle within a circle . . .

What to Do

Using the **circle()** function and your knowledge of filling in shapes with colors, draw one big circle and fill it with a color. Then, draw a medium-sized circle and fill it with a different color. At this point, make sure that you can still see the medium-sized circle and that it's contained within the big circle. Finally, draw one smaller circle, fill it with a different color, and make sure it is contained within the two larger circles.

Helpful Hints

Again, **for** loops will be your best friend in creating this drawing, as a lot of steps are repeated! First, keep track of each step you take to draw a circle and fill it with color. Once you have found the repeated steps, try moving it into a **for** loop. Then, figure out which parts you need to change to create different-sized circles and change colors.

Sample Expected Output

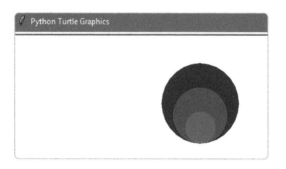

ACTIVITY 5: TOOGA'S HOUSE

Now that we know how to use the **turtle** module's built-in functions, let's create a proper home for Tooga!

What to Do

Create a new turtle named Tooga and a new pen to build Tooga's home:

```
tooga = turtle.Turtle()
pen = turtle.Turtle()
```

Using the **penup()** and **pendown()** functions, and changing colors and pen sizes, draw some shapes to create a house for Tooga. Make sure Tooga is actually inside the house you create for him!

This can be a simple square around Tooga with a triangle above the square to represent the roof. Get creative with the colors and pen sizes. Tooga would surely appreciate a non-boring, colorful home!

Helpful Hints

Use the **penup()** and **pendown()** functions to lift and drop the pen when you need to draw and not draw. This will make sure you don't draw on Tooga!

Sample Expected Output

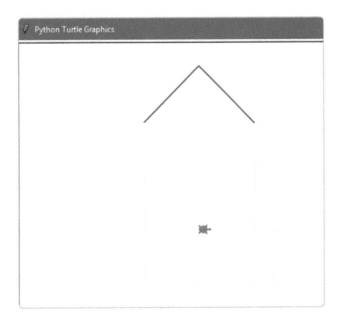

ACTIVITY 6: WRITING IN PYTHON

Use the **write()** function to write your name programmatically! Let's try it out!

What to Do

Using the **turtle** module's **write()** function, write your name on the screen!

```
turtle.write("Adrienne")
```

If you use the **write()** function's other parameters, you can change the way your text looks, including the font, size, and more. Here's an example:

```python
turtle.write("Adrienne", font = ("Freestyle Script",50,"normal"))
```

Helpful Hints

Search for other font names on your computer's word processing software, and change what your text looks like! If you want to change the color, be sure to change your turtle object's color first before using the **write()** function.

Sample Expected Output

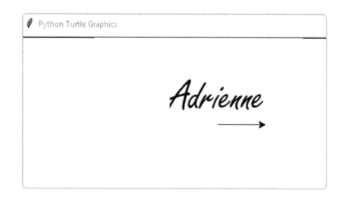

CHAPTER 6 ☆ CHALLENGES

- -

CHALLENGE 1: TOOGA'S TRAVELS

Every now and then, Tooga likes to go up to the surface of the water. He especially likes to go up during the night so he can see the stars! Sometimes he sees them when it's a clear night. If it's a cloudy night, however, there's not much to see, so he swims back down. Let's create a small program to draw some stars for Tooga, but only if it's a clear night!

What to Do

I've prepared some code for you to set the scene, so create a file called tooga-travels-activity and start including the following in that file:

```python
import turtle
import random

##### Start of setup #####
# Allow RGB values for colors
turtle.colormode(255)

# Set screen size and background color
turtle.Screen().setup(1000, 1000)
turtle.Screen().bgcolor(35, 58, 119)

# Draw a border to divide water and surface
divider_pen = turtle.Turtle()
divider_pen.color(255, 212, 31)
divider_pen.pensize(10)
divider_pen.back(500)
divider_pen.forward(1000)

# Hide pen after it is done drawing
divider_pen.ht()

# Create a pen to draw stars
pen = turtle.Turtle()

# Don't show its lines until we ask it to start drawing
pen.penup()

# Hide the pen as we only want to see Tooga!
pen.ht()

# Move the pen to the top left corner
pen.goto(-200,300)

# Set the pen's color and thickness
pen.color(255, 215, 0)
pen.pensize(5)

###### End of setup ######

###### Start of Tooga's Travels Activity #####

# Create a Tooga
tooga = turtle.Turtle()

# Make him a Turtle
<Write some code here>
```

MAY THE TURTLE BE WITH YOU

```python
# Make Tooga green, his outline dark green, and of medium size
tooga.color(9, 185, 13)
tooga.pencolor(0, 128, 0)
tooga.turtlesize(3, 3, 3)

# Hide any lines drawn from Tooga
tooga.penup()
tooga.goto(0, -100)

# Our function to draw a star

def draw_star():
    pen.pendown()

    # Use a for loop to repeat the
    # pen.forward(100) and pen.right(144) command
    # 5 times to draw a star
    <Write some code here>

    pen.penup()
    pen.goto(pen.xcor() + 200, pen.ycor() + 20)
return

tooga.left(90)

# Main Program
for i in range(1, 6):

    # Move Tooga forward 150 units
    <Write some code here>

    cloudy_night = random.choice([True, False])

    # Use a print function (and maybe an f-string)
    # to print out if it's a cloudy day or not
    <Write some code here>

    turtle.delay(30)

    # Use an if statement to check
    # it is NOT a cloudy night (AKA a clear night!)
    # If it is NOT a cloudy night, call your
    # draw_star() function
    <Write some code here>
```

```
# Turn Tooga to the right 180 units
<Write some code here>

# Move Tooga forward 150 units
<Write some code here>

turtle.delay(50)
tooga.right(180)
```

You'll see that I've left placeholders like this: **<Write some code here>** right where some important pieces of our program should be. When you find one, remove the comment and replace it with some code. Use your knowledge of **for** loops, the **turtle** module, and the **print()** function to finish the rest of the program.

Once you finish writing code for all of the missing parts, save your file! When you run it, you'll see something like this (Hint: It may vary, depending on how many times you have a cloudy night!):

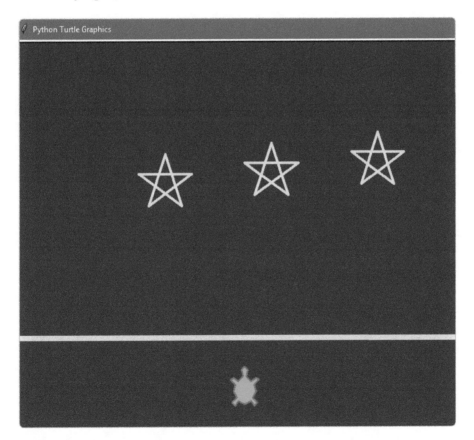

MAY THE TURTLE BE WITH YOU

Helpful Hints

The comments right above the placeholders will tell you what you need to do. Pay attention to the exact number, direction, coding block, or expression that is stated in the comments to keep your code on track!

CHALLENGE 2: MANDALA

Mandala is a Sanskrit word that means "circle." Some people like to draw really pretty and intricate mandalas with different colors and patterns. In this challenge, you'll test your knowledge of the **turtle** module and loops!

What to Do

Using your knowledge of loops and the **turtle** module, write a program to draw a mandala of your own. Use at least two colors and at least two different shapes or stamps.

CHALLENGE 3: MORE RAINBOW TURTLES!

Building on your Rainbow Turtles in Activity 3, see if you can move the turtles on your screen to draw an actual rainbow!

What to Do

Using the **circle()** function with all three parameters, draw different-sized semicircles for each color of the rainbow. Make sure all of your turtles are on the right side of the screen when you're finished drawing the rainbow!

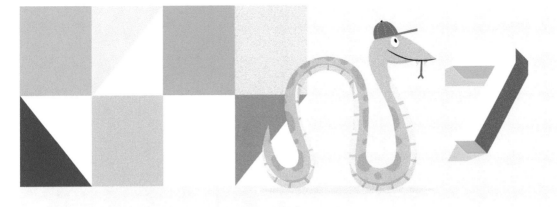

REUSABLE CODE

At the core of coding is the concept of *reusability*, or how easy it is to use something again and again. We write code that can do repetitive, complex, or time-consuming things for us, but if we had to write it *every* single time we needed to use it, coding wouldn't be very useful.

Functions and modules provide a way for us to write code that's reusable. If you think about it, we've already used so many in this book! We've used the **print()** function since chapter 1, and we've just learned about how fun and interactive the multipurpose **turtle** module is in chapter 6!

Most programs are made up of one or many modules, and each of those modules is usually made up of several functions. Let's see how writing code in this way helps us have smarter programs.

FUNCTIONS

As we've learned, functions are reusable blocks of code that can do something specific or return a value. Usually, we write functions for things that we often repeat. Let's say we needed to greet a person every time they used our program. We could write a **print()** function every single time we needed to greet them:

```python
print("Hello, person!")
print("Hello, person!")
print("Hello, person!")
```

Or, we could move this action of greeting a person into a function:

```python
def greet():
    print("Hello, person!")
```

which we can now use any time by writing code like this:

```
greet()
```

Here's what's happening: To create a function, we first need to describe what it will be called and what it will do. We start by using the **def** keyword, which signals to the computer that we are writing a function. It's short for define. Just like a dictionary defines what a word means, we define what our function will do when we use the **def** keyword.

Next, we name our function. Because we will be greeting people when we use this function, the name "greet" is a good choice, as it clearly describes what our function is doing. We then add some parentheses () to our function name. We may add parameters in the parentheses later, but for now, we don't have any. Lastly, a colon (:) shows that the following indented lines of code will be part of our function. That's it!

An important thing to know about functions is that they don't run on their own. This means that whenever a computer comes across one, it automatically skips the code within it. In order to actually use a function, it needs to be *called*, meaning we must clearly tell the computer to start executing the called function's code. If we don't call functions, the code within them will never be run!

PARAMETERS

Our **greet()** function is pretty normal. We say "Hello, person!" whenever we call it. But what if we wanted to greet the person by their name, instead of the word "person?" That would be a much nicer greeting, wouldn't it? Parameters are just the thing we need to add to our function in order to do this! A *parameter* is a piece of input data we give to a function to do something with. A function can have no parameters, just like our original **greet()** function, or it can have one or more parameters. When we create functions that use parameters, we say that these functions accept parameters, which lets us know that the function can take pieces of input data.

To make our **greet()** function a little nicer, let's have it accept one parameter called **name** and then use it in our greeting! We add a parameter to a function by placing it in between the parentheses that come after the function name, like this:

```
def greet(name):
    print("Hello, person!")
```

By adding this parameter to the function, we are now able to use it within our function. This means we can do something like this:

```python
def greet(name):
    print(f"Hello, {name}!")
```

Now, when we call our **greet()** function, it will use the parameter you pass into it, meaning this code:

```python
greet("Adrienne")
```

will result in this output:

```python
'Hello, Adrienne!'
```

Pretty cool! You know what, though? We can make our **greet()** function even cooler. Let's decide that we not only want to greet someone by their name, but that we also want to change our greeting depending on the person. We might say, "What's up, Adrienne? Nice to see you again!" if we are greeting someone we know very well, or "Hello, Duke! Nice to meet you!" if it's someone new.

Remember, code is all about reusability, so we're already ahead of the game by putting our greeting into a function. We just have to change it a little bit to do these other things we mentioned! To start, let's add another parameter to our **greet()** function. We'll add a parameter called **is_new**, which can tell the function whether the person we are greeting is someone we know:

```python
def greet(name, is_new):
    print(f"Hello, {name}!")
```

Great! Now, we just need to add some logic to our function. Remember, we want to print a different greeting for the people we know than the one we print for the people we don't know. In this case, we can use our newly added **is_new** parameter to help us make this decision! So, if we don't know the person, we can use a specific greeting:

```python
def greet(name, is_new):
    if(is_new):
        print(f"Hello, {name}! Nice to meet you!")
```

Otherwise, we'll use the friendlier greeting:

```python
def greet(name, is_new):
    if(is_new):
        print(f"Hello, {name}! Nice to meet you!")
```

REUSABLE CODE

```
    else:
        print(f"What's up, {name}? Nice to see you again!")
```

That's it! Now, when we use our **greet()** function, we just need to pass in a few inputs for the parameters, and it can do the rest of the work for us! Using the parameters we pass in, the computer can decide which greeting to use. We can also call our **greet()** function as many times as we want, and it will print out a greeting every time.

```
Python 3.7.0 Shell                                              —    □    ×

File  Edit  Shell  Debug  Options  Window  Help
Python 3.7.0 (v3.7.0:1bf9cc5093, Jun 27 2018, 04:59:51) [MSC v.1914 64 bit (AMD6 ^
4)] on win32
Type "copyright", "credits" or "license()" for more information.
>>> def greet(name, is_new):
        if(is_new):
                print(f"Hello, {name}! Nice to meet you!")
        else:
                print(f"What's up, {name}? Nice to see you again!")


>>> greet("Adrienne", False)
What's up, Adrienne? Nice to see you again!
>>> greet("Duke", True)
Hello, Duke! Nice to meet you!
>>> greet("Mario", False)
What's up, Mario? Nice to see you again!
>>> greet("Eva", True)
Hello, Eva! Nice to meet you!
>>> greet("Coco", True)
Hello, Coco! Nice to meet you!
>>> greet("Bernard", False)
What's up, Bernard? Nice to see you again!
>>>
```

Can you imagine having to write an **if** statement and print a different f-string each time you needed to do this greeting? Functions make it much easier and smarter to do actions like this in code!

RETURN VALUES

As we've seen, functions are great for actions we need to repeat. We can use them to do something for us once or 100 times, depending on how many times we need it. Functions are also good at helping us perform calculations or make some changes to data before we can continue using it in our code. These kinds of functions usually have *return values*, which is the resulting output a function gives us back after calling it.

We've already used many functions that return some data to us throughout this book. If you look back to the **turtle** module, we used the **xcor()** and **ycor()** functions (page 148). Do you remember what return values they gave back? When called, these functions returned the current x coordinate and current y coordinate of our turtle!

CODING FOR KIDS : PYTHON

Function	Input/Parameters Accepted	Output/Return Value
xcor()	none	x coordinate of turtle
ycor()	none	y coordinate of turtle

How about the **range()** function? When we talked about loops, we used the **range()** function to iterate through specific ranges of numbers. This function accepted a starting and stopping index (our input parameters). The **range()** function then takes these parameters and creates a list of all the numbers that are between these starting and stopping indices. This newly created list of numbers is then returned to us (our return value) so we can iterate through it in the loop we originally called it in.

Function	Input/Parameters Accepted	Output/Return Value
range(stop)	stopping index **ex:** range(5)	List of numbers from 0 to stopping index
range(start, stop)	starting index, stopping index **ex:** range(1, 10)	List of numbers from starting index to stopping index
range(start, stop, step)	Starting index, stopping index, step **ex:** range(1, 100, 5)	List of numbers from starting index to stopping index, but by step amount

CALLING FUNCTIONS

Calling a function is easy! Whenever there is a point in your code that you need to use a function, simply call it by writing the function name followed by parentheses ():

greet()

That's it! This is the way we call functions that are in the same file.

REUSABLE CODE

Functions in Other Files

You'll notice that we have already been calling many functions throughout this book that we haven't defined ourselves. These include functions like the **print()** function and many of the ones provided by the built-in Python modules. All of these functions are located in different files, yet we can still use them. How?

When we want to call functions that are in other files, we have to make sure they are available for the computer to use in our code. Fun fact: We already know how to do this, and we did it in chapter 6 with the **turtle** module! Can you guess how? If you said importing, then you're correct!

Just as we imported the entire **turtle** module in our files in chapter 6 so we could use all parts of the module, we can import only the specific functions that we want to use. Let's say we have a file called colors.py, and in it, we've defined the following functions:

```python
def rgb_red():
    return (255, 0, 0)

def rgb_green():
    return (0, 255, 0)

def rgb_blue():
    return (0, 0, 255)

def purple():
    return "red + blue"

def yellow():
    return "blue + green"

def orange():
    return "red + yellow"
```

Later on, we decide to create a game that deals with colors. We create another file to hold our game and call it color-game.py. Knowing we have some functions that we can reuse from the colors.py file, we decide to import them into our color game. For our purposes, we only need the **rgb_red()**, **purple()**, and **yellow()** functions from this file. Instead of importing the entire colors file, we can import just the functions we need, like this:

```python
from colors import rgb_red, purple, yellow
```

Simple, right? The code even makes sense when you read it out loud. We pretty much tell the computer, "Hey, I need some functions from the colors file, but I only need the **rgb_red()**, **purple()**, and **yellow()** functions. Can you bring those into my file so I can use them? Thanks!"

TO HAVE PARENTHESES OR TO NOT HAVE PARENTHESES

When we import specific functions from a module or file, you'll notice that we write their names without the parentheses:

```
from colors import rgb_red, purple, yellow
```

This is correct! Remember, if we place parentheses after a function name, it is the same as calling the function, which means executing the function's code. We don't want to do that just yet—we simply want to make them available in the file we are importing them into. Keep this in mind as you import functions into your files.

Now, when you write more code in your color game file, you'll be able to call the **rgb_red()**, **purple()**, and **yellow()** functions!

CODE COMPLETE!

We learned a lot about writing our own code and using it with other shared code in the Python language!

- We learned what **functions** are and how they make up most modules and programs.

- We learned how to create our own functions.

- We went over functions with and without parameters.

- We discussed what **return values** are.

- We learned how to call our functions in other parts of our code.

- We learned how to import full modules or only the parts we need for our own code.

    You're pretty much a coder now! How does it feel?

157

REUSABLE CODE

CHAPTER 7 ★ ACTIVITIES

ACTIVITY 1: SUPER FUNCTION!

What to Do

Create a function called **superpower()**. Have your **superpower()** function accept two parameters: one called **name** and another called **power**. Using these parameters, have your function print out an f-string that says who you are and what your superpower is!

Sample Expected Output

```
'Hi, I'm Super Adrienne and my superpower is coding!'
```

ACTIVITY 2: FUNNY FUNCTIONS

What to Do

Create a function called **funny_greeting()**. Have your **funny_greeting()** function accept two parameters: one called **color** and another called **dessert**. Using these parameters, have your function print out an f-string that mixes up the parameters on purpose to produce a silly message!

Sample Expected Output

```
'My favorite dessert is red because it tastes so good, and my favorite
color is blueberry pie because it is very pretty!!'
```

ACTIVITY 3: WHAT TIME IS IT OVER THERE?

When you have friends around the world, it can get a little tricky to keep track of the right times to call them. Depending on where they are, they can be hours ahead of or behind the time in your location! To help, let's write a function that helps us figure out what time it is in our friends' cities.

CODING FOR KIDS : PYTHON

What to Do

Using the **datetime()** and **timedelta()** functions from the **datetime** module (see page 215) and some math, write a function that prints out the current time in your home city and the following three cities:

Berlin, Germany
Baguio City, Philippines
Tokyo, Japan
My Home: **Las Vegas, United States**

First, be sure to import the following functions so you can use them:

```
from datetime import datetime
from datetime import timedelta
```

Next, create a function called **world_times()**. I've already started the function for you, so just fill in the blanks to calculate the other cities' times and then print out the final string!

```
def world_times():

    my_city = datetime.now()
    berlin = <Write some code here>
    baguio = <Write some code here>
    tokyo = <Write some code here>
    all_times = f'''It is {my_city:%I:%M} in my city.

That means it's {berlin:%I:%M} in Berlin, {baguio:%I:%M} in Baguio
City and {tokyo:%I:%M} in Tokyo!'''

<Write some code here> # print your all_times variable!
```

To calculate the other cities' times, you'll probably need to add some hours to the **my_city** variable. You can add hours to a variable by using the **timedelta()** function. The **timedelta()** function gives us an easy way to properly add units of time (like days, months, hours, minutes, etc.) to a date or time.

In this activity, you'll only need to add hours. You do this by adding a **datetime** object to a specific amount of hours. So as an example, if you wanted to add 9 hours to the current time and then assign this result to a variable called **nine_hours_from_now**, you'd do the following:

```
nine_hours_from_now = datetime.now() + timedelta(hours=9)
```

>>> **HELPFUL HINT:** You can use the Internet to find the time differences between your home city and the three cities mentioned. Once you figure out those numbers, use them in your function's calculations!

>>> **HELPFUL HINT:** Don't change the f-string I've provided! The resulting times you calculate should print out to a nice, readable format.

Sample Expected Output

```
>>> world_times()

It is 07:37 in Las Vegas.

That means it's 04:37 in Berlin, 10:37 in Baguio City, and 11:37
in Tokyo!
```

ACTIVITY 4: FACTORIAL FUNCTION

One of the most common functions every coder has to write is called a *factorial* function. It's a function that calculates the factorial of the number you pass into it. And yes, it sounds like something to do with multiplication, because it is! In math, a factorial is the product of a number and all the numbers that come before it. So, if I asked you to calculate the factorial of the number 4, you would have to multiply 4 * 3 * 2 * 1. The factorial of 4 is 24.

What to Do

Write a function called **factorial()** that takes one parameter. This parameter will be a number. Then, write the code to calculate the factorial of the number that is passed in as a parameter. Have your **factorial()** function return the answer!

Sample Expected Output

```
>>> factorial(4)

24
```

ACTIVITY 5: CUPCAKECOOKIE

Dolores and Maeve are having a party together and are setting up the dessert tables. Dolores likes cupcakes and Maeve loves cookies! Unfortunately, when they go to the kitchen, all of their boxes have been mixed up! Each dessert is in a special box, but all the boxes look the same! Dolores and Maeve don't fret, though. They know that they can tell which dessert is which, because the cookies are in a box with a 3 on them and the cupcakes are in a box with a 5. Let's write a function to help them organize their desserts!

What to Do

Write a function called **dessert_sorter()** that takes one parameter. Call the parameter **total_desserts**. Then, write some code that will help Dolores and Maeve separate the cupcakes from the cookies. This should be a **for** loop that goes through the **total_desserts** and checks for these things:

• If it's a number that's divisible by 3, print out the word "cupcake."

• If it's a number that's divisible by 5, print out the word "cookie."

• If it's a number that's divisible by both 3 and 5, print out "it's a cupcakecookie!"

When you're done creating your **dessert_sorter()** function, pass in 200 as the **total_desserts** parameter, because that's how many boxes Dolores and Maeve have to sort!

Sample Expected Output

```
>>> dessert_sorter(15)
cupcake
cookie
cupcake
cupcake
cookie
cupcake
it's a cupcakecookie!
```

161

ACTIVITY 6: DRAWING GAME BOARDS

A lot of games require a game board made up of a different number of squares. Let's try creating a module that creates any size game board we need by simply giving it a number!

What to Do

Create a file called game-board and save it. Then, define two functions: one to print some horizontal lines and one to print some vertical lines:

```
def print_horizontal_line():
def print_vertical_line():
```

Next, use the **print()** function to print out the lines:

```
def print_horizontal_line():
    print(" --- ")

def print_vertical_line():
    print("|  _ ")
```

Next, we need to ask the player what size game board they need. We should capture their input in a variable:

```
board_size = int(input("What size game board do you need?"))
```

Finally, create a **for** loop that iterates as many times as the board size requested by the player, and print the lines using your defined print line functions!

```
<Write some code here>
```

Now, to correctly print the game board, we need to change our print line functions a bit. For the **print_horizontal_line()** function, how would you change it to print as many lines as the requested game board size? (Hint: Remember that weird operator that we can use to "multiply" strings? Hmm ...)

```
def print_horizontal_line():
    print(" --- " <Write some code here>)
```

For the **print_vertical_line()** function, you'll need to print out as many lines as the requested board size, plus one.

```
def print_vertical_line():
    print("|  _   " <Write some code here>)
```

Finally, print one last horizontal line to finish your board after your **for** loop:

```
print(" --- " * board_size)
```

That's it! When you save and run your file, it will ask you what size board you need. Give it a number, and it will print out a board for you, making the board that number of squares high and wide. As you can see here, the number 3 gave us a board three squares wide and three squares high!

Sample Expected Output

```
Python 3.7.0 Shell                                          —   □   ×
File  Edit  Shell  Debug  Options  Window  Help
>>>
======= RESTART: C:/Users/Adrienne/Documents/Cool Python/game-board.py =======
What size of game board? 3
 ---  ---  ---
|    |    |    |       |
 ---  ---  ---
|    |    |    |
 ---  ---  ---
|    |    |    |
 ---  ---  ---
>>>
                                                        Ln: 249  Col: 20
```

ACTIVITY 7: ROCK PAPER SCISSORS

Rock, paper, scissors, go! This game is a very popular game to play with friends. For as many turns that you like, you and a friend can choose between rock, paper, or scissors and see who wins between the two of you. Let's create this game in Python, where you can battle friends on the computer!

What to Do

Create a file called rock-paper-scissors-game, and save it. Next, begin creating your game!

Let's start by greeting the players:

```
print("Welcome to the Rock Paper Scissors Game!")
```

Now, create two variables that will store the names of each player

```
player_1 = <Write some code here>
player_2 = <Write some code here>
```

Next, define a function called **compare()** and have it accept two parameters. This function will compare the players' choices (which are the two parameters it accepts) and tell us who won, based on the rules of Rock Paper Scissors:

```
def compare(item_1, item_2):
```

Now, within our **compare()** function, we have to write a few **if** statements! Check for each combination possible in Rock Paper Scissors, and then print out the winner in each combination. Keep in mind that each item is stronger than one other item but weaker than another. To help you write the Boolean expressions for your **if** statements, I've provided a list of Rock Paper Scissors combinations and who would win in each combination, based on the rules:

Choice 1	Choice 2	Winner Between the Two
Rock	Paper	Paper (paper covers rock)
Rock	Scissors	Rock (rock breaks scissors)
Rock	Rock	It's a tie!
Paper	Rock	Paper (paper covers rock)
Paper	Scissors	Scissors (scissors cut paper)
Paper	Paper	It's a tie!
Scissors	Rock	Rock (rock breaks scissors)
Scissors	Paper	Scissors (scissors cut paper)
Scissors	Scissors	It's a tie!

Be sure to add one last **elif** statement to deal with any choices that are not rock, paper, or scissors! It would be a good idea to also tell the players that they have entered a choice that is not possible if they do this.

Now that we have a **compare()** function that can check the combinations for us, the last part is to actually capture the choices our players choose! Create two variables to store the player's choices:

```
player_1_choice = <Write some code here>
player_2_choice = <Write some code here>
```

Lastly, use a **print()** function to print the results of the **compare()** function when you pass the players' choices into it!

```
print(compare(player_1_choice, player_2_choice))
```

That's it! Save your file, then press F5 to run it so you can play Rock Paper Scissors with a friend! Take turns entering your choices, and see who's won!

CHAPTER 7 ☆ CHALLENGES

CHALLENGE 1: HANGMAN GAME

Using everything you have learned, try finishing this hangman game. I have provided the structure for a hangman game below for you to use. However, it's up to you to fill in the blanks! Once you have filled in all of the missing code, noted by the **<Write some code here>** placeholders, save your file. At this point, you should be able to play hangman when you press **F5** and run your game!

What to Do

Create a new file called hangman, and save it. Using the template below, start writing the code into your own hangman.py file. When you come to a placeholder that says **<Write some code here>**, remove the placeholder and replace it with the proper code. Use the comments to help you figure out what kind of code to write.

```
# importing the time module
import time

# Welcome the user and capture their name in a name variable
name = input("What is your name?")

# Use a print function to greet the user by their name
<Write some code here>

# Wait for 1 second
time.sleep(1)

print("Start guessing...")
time.sleep(0.5)

# Create a variable called secret_word to store the word to be guessed
```

165

```
<Write some code here>

# Create a variable called guesses and assign it to an empty string ''
# We'll store the letters the player guesses here
<Write some code here>

# Create a variable to store the maximum number of turns the game
will allow
<Write some code here>

# Start a while loop
# and check if we have more than 0 turns available
<Write some code here>

    # If we have turns available:
    # Create a counter variable that starts at 0 to hold the number of
    incorrect
    # guesses we make
    <Write some code here>

    # Start a for loop
    # and iterate through every character in your secret_word variable
    <Write some code here>

            # As you iterate through each character:
            # use an if statement to check if the letter is
            # in the player's guess, aka the guesses variable
            <Write some code here>
                # If it is, print then out the character
                <Write some code here>
            else:
                # If it isn't, print an underscore ...
                 print("_")

                # ...and increase the failed counter by 1
                <Write some code here>
```

```
# Check if your incorrect guesses are equal to 0
<Write some code here>

    # If it is, tell the user they've won!
     <Write some code here>

    # ...then exit the game
    break

# Otherwise, ask the player to guess another character
guess = input("Guess a character:")

# Add the player's guess to the guesses variable
guesses += guess

# Create an if statement
# and check if the guess is not found in the word
<Write some code here>

    # Decrease your turns by 1
    <Write some code here>

    # ...and tell the player their guess was wrong
    <Write some code here>

    # Also tell the player how many turns they have left
    <Write some code here>

    # Create an if statement to check if your turns are
    equal to 0
    <Write some code here>

        # If they are, tell the player they've lost
        <Write some code here>
```

REUSABLE CODE

CHALLENGE 2: TURTLE RACE!

Let's race some Toogas! We'll create a race track and some colorful turtles, and then send them off! Play with your friends by choosing a turtle at the beginning of the race and seeing if it finishes first!

What to Do

Create a new file called turtle-race-game, and save it. Then, begin coding your turtle race game!

First, import the **turtle** and **random** modules like this:

```
from turtle import *
from random import randint
```

Next, let's set up the race track:

```
speed()
penup()
goto(-140, 140)

# Create a for loop that iterates from 0 - 15
<Write some code here>

    # Use the write() function to write the number of your for loop
    iterator.
    # Set the align parameter to 'center'. These will be your steps or
    distances
    # in the race!
    <Write some code here>

    right(90)

    # Create another for loop that iterates from 0 - 8
    <Write some code here>

        # Use the penup(), forward(), and pendown() functions
        # to draw dashes for your race track

        # First, lift your pen
        <Write some code here>
```

```python
        # Second, move forward 10 pixels
        <Write some code here>
        # Third, put your pen down
        <Write some code here>
        # Last, move forward another 10 pixels
        <Write some code here>


    # Go backward so you can draw the dashes
    # for the other steps/distances

    # First, lift your pen
    <Write some code here>
    # Then, move backward 160 pixels
    <Write some code here>
    # Turn left 90 degrees
    <Write some code here>
    # Last, move forward 20 pixels
    <Write some code here>

# Now, begin creating turtles! I'll create four, but feel free to
create more

# Create a turtle
<Write some code here>

# Set its shape to a turtle
<Write some code here>

# Set its color
<Write some code here>

# Lift your pen
<Write some code here>

# Now, move this first turtle to the top left
# Use the goto() function to move it to x = -160, y = 100
<Write some code here>

# Put the pen back down
<Write some code here>
```

```
# Finally, make your first turtle do a little spin
# when they get to the starting line!

# Create a for loop that iterates from zero to a number you choose
<Write some code here>

    # Turn your first turtle to the right by a number of degrees
    you choose
    <Write some code here>

# Create three (or more!) turtles with different names and colors
# Make sure each turtle repeats all of the steps and code we wrote
# for the first turtle :)
#
# When you get to the goto() function for each turtle
# use these coordinates:
# 2nd turtle: x = -160, y = 70
# 3rd turtle: x = -160, y = 40
# 4th turtle: x = -160, y = 10
# any other turtle afterward: x = -160, y = the last turtle's y coor-
dinate minus 30

<Write lots of code here>
<Code for the three other turtles>

# Finally, after your code for three other turtles,
# make the turtles race!

# Create a for loop that iterates 100 times
<Write some code here>

    # For each turtle, move them forward by a random number
    # chosen by the random function. Give the random function
    # a range of 1 - 5 to pick from
    <Write some code here>
```

That's it! Save your game, pick a turtle, and press F5 to run your game. You'll get to watch your race track be drawn and all of your turtles race!

CODING FOR KIDS : PYTHON

FINAL BITS AND BYTES

What Will You Build?

Congratulations, coder! You've officially learned how to code in the Python language!

We've learned how to download and install Python so you can code on any computer. We covered the basic building blocks of programming, from the `print()` function and the main data types, to smarter code blocks and decision-making in code. Toward the end, we played with the **turtle** module and learned how to draw and move shapes. Finally, we learned about the importance of making code reusable through functions and modules, and explored how we can combine many of the building blocks we've learned to create our own. We covered a lot of ground and did a lot of thinking, so you should be proud!

Now that you have the proper tools and knowledge for coding in Python, what will you build? We've created a few games and have gone through some silly and fun activities, so those are just a starting point. But there is so much more that you can do. How about building your own game? Or writing a small program to create nice pictures and messages for your friends? What if you created a small program to help someone in need? The possibilities are endless . . . . You just have to imagine it—then code it!

ANSWER KEY

As an additional resource, this answer key provides sample code solutions for the activities and challenges outlined in this book. Keep in mind: these code samples are just one way of achieving the end result! They are not the only solutions, nor are they the "correct" or "best" solutions. There are plenty of ways to write code to achieve the same results, so be sure to give an honest try before using the code samples here!

CHAPTER 2 ★ ACTIVITIES

ACTIVITY 1: INTRODUCE YOURSELF

Possible Solution

```
print("Hi! My name is Adrienne.")
```

ACTIVITY 2: TO QUOTE A QUOTE

Possible Solution

```
print("\"First, solve the problem. Then, write the code.\" - John
Johnson")
```

ACTIVITY 3: MOOD IS VARIABLE

Possible Solution

```
mood = "curious"
print(f"Today, I feel {mood}!")
```

ACTIVITY 4: HAIKU, ABOUT YOU!

Possible Solution

```
haiku = """
    Adrienne enjoys
    Coffee, lots of coding, and
    Teaching you Python
"""
print(f"{haiku}")
```

Alternative solution

```
haiku = """
    Adrienne enjoys
    Coffee, lots of coding, and
    Teaching you Python
"""

print(haiku)
```

ACTIVITY 5: SILLY STORIES

Possible Solution

```
name = ""
adjective = ""
favorite_snack = ""
number = ""
type_of_tree = ""

silly_story = f"""
    Hi, my name is {name}.
    I really like {adjective} {favorite_snack}!
    I like it so much, I try to eat at least {number} every day.
    It tastes even better when you eat it under a {type_of_tree}!
"""

print(silly_story)
```

ACTIVITY 6: REUSABLE VARIABLES

Possible Solution

```
first_name = 'Adrienne'
full_name = f"{first_name} Tacke"

print(full_name)
```

Possible Solutions

```
first_name = "Adrienne"
favorite_snack = "Chocolate chip cookies"
age = 20
favorite_color = "Blue"
full_name = "Adrienne Tacke"
occupation = "Software Engineer"

print(f"{first_name} {favorite_snack} {age} {favorite_color}
{full_name} {occupation}")
```

CHAPTER 2 ★ CHALLENGES

CHALLENGE 1: MULTILAYER CAKE

Possible Solution

```
cake = '''
  @@@@@
  {   }
 @@@@@@@
 {     }
@@@@@@@@@
{       }
'''

print(cake)
```

CHAPTER 3 ★ ACTIVITIES

ACTIVITY 1: HOW OLD ARE YOU?

Possible Solution

```
name = "Adrienne"
age = 20 + 7

print(f"Hi! My name is {name} and I am {age} years old!")
```

175

ANSWER KEY

ACTIVITY 2: OPERATION PEMDAS

Possible Solution

```
magic_number = (5 ** 3 + 175) + (27 % 4) * 11
```

ACTIVITY 3: COOKIE COMPARISONS

Possible Solution

Rey & Finn

Rey says she has less than or equal to the number of chocolate chips as Finn.

```
rey_chocolate_chips = 10
finn_chocolate_chips = 18
print(f"Rey's cookie has less than or the same amount of
chocolate chips as Finn's. This is {rey_chocolate_chips <=
finn_chocolate_chips}!")
```

Possible Solution

Tom & Jerry

Tom says he does not have the same amount of chocolate chips in his cookie as Jerry.

```
tom_chocolate_chips = 50
jerry_chocolate_chips = "50"
print(f"Tom's cookie does not have the same amount of chocolate chips
as Jerry's. This is {tom_chocolate_chips != jerry_chocolate_chips}!")
```

Possible Solution

Trinity & Neo

Neo says he has the same number of chocolate chips as Trinity.

```
neo_chocolate_chips = 3
trinity_chocolate_chips = 3
print(f"Neo's cookie has the same amount of chocolate chips as
Trinity's. This is {neo_chocolate_chips == trinity_chocolate_chips}!")
```

ANSWER KEY

Possible Solution

Gigi & Kiki

Kiki says she has less chocolate chips in her cookie than Gigi.

```
kiki_chocolate_chips = 30
gigi_chocolate_chips = 31
print(f"Kiki's cookie has less chocolate chips than Gigi's. This is
{kiki_chocolate_chips < gigi_chocolate_chips}!")
```

Possible Solution

Bernard & Elsie

Bernard says he has at least the same amount of chocolate chips as Elsie, maybe even more!

```
bernard_chocolate_chips = 1010
elsie_chocolate_chips = 10101
print(f"Bernard's cookie has the same amount of chocolate chips
or more than Elsie's. This is {bernard_chocolate_chips >=
elsie_chocolate_chips}!")
```

ACTIVITY 4: PIE PARTY!

Possible Solution

Chocolate and Caramel Pie

```
pie_crust = "graham cracker"
pie_slices = 10
can_evenly_divide_chocolate_caramel_pie = (graham_cracker_crust_lovers
% 10) == 0
print(f"The Chocolate and Caramel pie can be evenly divided for all
graham crust lovers? {can_evenly_divide_chocolate_caramel_pie}")
```

Possible Solution

Triple Berry Pie

```
pie_crust = "vanilla wafer"
pie_slices = 12
```

ANSWER KEY

```
can_evenly_divide_triple_berry_pie = (vanilla_wafer_crust_lovers %
12) == 0

print(f"The Triple Berry pie can be evenly divided for all vanilla
wafer crust lovers? {can_evenly_divide_triple_berry_pie }")
```

Possible Solution

Pumpkin Pie
```
pie_crust = "graham cracker"
pie_slices = 12
can_evenly_divide_pumpkin_pie = (graham_cracker_crust_lovers %
12) == 0
print(f"The Pumpkin pie can be evenly divided for all graham crust
lovers? {can_evenly_divide_pumpkin_pie}")
```

Possible Solution

Apple Pie
```
pie_crust = "vanilla wafer"
pie_slices = 10
can_evenly_divide_apple_pie = (vanilla_wafer_crust_lovers % 10) == 0
print(f"The Apple pie can be evenly divided for all vanilla wafer
crust lovers? {can_evenly_divide_apple_pie}")
```

Possible Solution

Banana Cream Pie
```
pie_crust = "vanilla wafer"
pie_slices = 10
can_evenly_divide_banana_cream_pie = (vanilla_wafer_crust_lovers %
10) == 0
print(f"The Banana Cream pie can be evenly divided for all vanilla
wafer crust lovers? {can_evenly_divide_banana_cream_pie}")
```

Possible Solution

Mango Pie

```
pie_crust = "graham cracker"
pie_slices = 12
can_evenly_divide_mango_pie = (graham_cracker_crust_lovers % 12) == 0
print(f"The Mango pie can be evenly divided for all graham crust
lovers? {can_evenly_divide_mango_pie}")
```

Possible Solution

S'mores Pie

```
pie_crust = "oreo"
pie_slices = 12
can_evenly_divide_smores_pie = (oreo_crust_wafers % 12) == 0
print(f"The S'mores pie can be evenly divided for all oreo crust
lovers? {can_evenly_divide_smores_pie}")
```

ACTIVITY 5: OUTFIT CHECKER

```
cher_dress_color = 'pink'
cher_shoe_color = 'white'
cher_has_earrings = True
dionne_dress_color = 'purple'
dionne_shoe_color = 'pink'
dionne_has_earrings = True
```

Possible Solution

Outfit Check 1

Cher and Dionne have different dress colors.

```
print(f"Both girls have different dress colors? {cher_dress_color !=
'purple' and dionne_dress_color != 'pink'}")
```

ANSWER KEY

Possible Solution

Outfit Check 2
Cher and Dionne are both wearing earrings.

```
print(f"Both girls are wearing earrings? {cher_has_earrings == True
and dionne_has_earrings == True}")
```

Possible Solution

Outfit Check 3
At least one person is wearing pink.

```
print(f"At least one person is wearing pink? {cher_dress_color ==
'pink' or dionne_dress_color == 'pink'}")
```

Possible Solution

Outfit Check 4
No one is wearing green.

```
print(f"No one is wearing green? {cher_dress_color != 'green' and
dionne_dress_color != 'green'}")
```

Possible Solution

Outfit Check 5
Cher and Dionne have the same shoe color.

```
print(f"Both girls have the same shoe colors? {(cher_shoe_color ==
'pink' and dionne_shoe_color == 'pink') or (cher_shoe_color == 'white'
and dionne_shoe_color == 'white')}")
```

ACTIVITY 6: LOGICAL LAB!

Possible Solution

```
beakers = 20
tubes = 30
rubber_gloves = 10
safety_glasses = 4
```

ANSWER KEY

```
enough_safety_glasses = (safety_glasses % 4) == 0
enough_rubber_gloves = rubber_gloves >= (2 * 4)
enough_tubes = tubes >= 10 * 4
enough_beakers = beakers >= 5 * 4

final_report = f'''
    Here is the final report for lab materials:
    -
    Each girl had enough safety glasses: {enough_safety_glasses}
    Each girl had enough rubber gloves: {enough_rubber_gloves }
    Each girl had enough tubes: {enough_tubes}
    Each girl had enough beakers: {enough_beakers}
    -
    There are enough gloves and safety glasses for each girl:
    {enough_rubber_gloves and enough_safety_glasses}
    There are more than enough tubes and an exact amount of beakers for
    each girl: {tubes > 40 and beakers == 20}
    Each girl has at least the exact or greater amount of tubes or the
    exact amount of beakers: {tubes >= 40 or beakers == 20}

'''

print(final_report)
```

ACTIVITY 7: MODULUS MATH

Possible Solution

```
print(3921 % 4)
print(533 % 7)
```

ACTIVITY 8: PLANETARY EXPONENTIATION

Possible Solution

Tripolia galaxy - magic number is 3!

```
print(f"The Tripolia galaxy has { 9 ** 3 } planets!")
```

Possible Solution

Deka galaxy - magic number is 10!

```python
print(f"The Deka galaxy has { 9 ** 10 } planets!")
```

Possible Solution

Heptaton galaxy - magic number is 7!

```python
print(f"The Heptaton galaxy has { 9 ** 7 } planets!")
```

Possible Solution

Oktopia galaxy - magic number is 8!

```python
print(f"The Oktopia galaxy has { 9 ** 8 } planets!")
```

CHAPTER 3 ⭐ CHALLENGES

- -

CHALLENGE 1: DINNER DECISIONS

```python
name = "Adrienne"
entree = fried_chicken
side_one = french_fries
side_two = baked_potato
dessert_one = chocolate_ice_cream
dessert_two = apple_pie
dessert_three = vanilla_donut
dinner_decisions = f"""
    Hi, my name is {name}.
    I chose {entree} as my main meal!
    To go with it, I chose {side_one}, {side_two} as my sides.
    And the best part, I have {dessert_one}, {dessert_two}, and
    {dessert_three} waiting for me for dessert!
    Let's eat!
"""

print(dinner_decisions)
```

CHAPTER 4 ☆ ACTIVITIES

ACTIVITY 1: THESE ARE A FEW OF MY FAVORITE THINGS

Possible Solution

```
my_favorite_things = ['Blue', 3, 'Desserts', 'Running', 33.3]
print(f"These are Adrienne's favorite things: {my_favorite_things}")
```

ACTIVITY 2: SHAPESHIFTERS

Possible Solution

```
your_cloud_shapes = ['circle', 'turtle', 'dolphin', 'truck', 'apple',
'spoon']

friend_cloud_shapes = ['apple', 'turtle', 'spoon', 'truck', 'circle',
'dolphin']

if your_cloud_shapes[0] == friend_cloud_shapes[0]:
    print("We saw the same shape!")
elif your_cloud_shapes[0] != friend_cloud_shapes[0]:
     print("We saw different shapes this time.")

if your_cloud_shapes[1] == friend_cloud_shapes[1]:
    print("We saw the same shape!")
elif your_cloud_shapes[1] != friend_cloud_shapes[1]:
    print("We saw different shapes this time.")

if your_cloud_shapes[2] == friend_cloud_shapes[2]:
    print("We saw the same shape!")
elif your_cloud_shapes[2] != friend_cloud_shapes[2]:
    print("We saw different shapes this time.")

if your_cloud_shapes[3] == friend_cloud_shapes[3]:
    print("We saw the same shape!")
elif your_cloud_shapes[3] != friend_cloud_shapes[3]:
    print("We saw different shapes this time.")
```

ANSWER KEY

```
if your_cloud_shapes[4] == friend_cloud_shapes[4]:
    print("We saw the same shape!")
elif your_cloud_shapes[4] != friend_cloud_shapes[4]:
    print("We saw different shapes this time.")

if your_cloud_shapes[5] == friend_cloud_shapes[5]:
    print("We saw the same shape!")
elif your_cloud_shapes[5] != friend_cloud_shapes[5]:
    print("We saw different shapes this time.")
```

ACTIVITY 3: RANDOM FACTORY

Scenario 1

Andre is about to play tennis with some friends. He has his tennis racket, but he needs one more thing. Write some code to print out what he needs!

Possible Solution

```
print(f"{random_items[1]} {random_items[4]}")
```

Scenario 2

Jean just baked some fresh bread. He wants to bring a few loaves home to share. What can you make from the random items list that can help him carry his bread home?

Possible Solution

```
print(f"{random_items[2]} {random_items[0]}")
```

Scenario 3

Christina is singing the words to a popular song that is usually sung at a baseball game. Can you finish the lyrics? "Take me out to the _____ _____ !"

ANSWER KEY

Possible Solution

```
print(f"{random_items[4]} {random_items[5]}")
```

Scenario 4

Leslie is writing a story on her favorite sport. It involves a hoop, five players on each team, and a recognizable orange ball with black stripes. Which sport is it?

Possible Solution

```
print(f"{random_items[0]} {random_items[4]}")
```

Scenario 5

Julia just received one of the fresh loaves of bread from Jean. Thanking him, she quickly puts the loaf she received in this item to keep it warm.

Possible Solution

```
print(f"{random_items[2]} {random_items[6]}")
```

Scenario 6

Mario has a lot of board games and video games. Luckily, he can store most of them in this item to keep his room nice and clean!

Possible Solution

```
print(f"{random_items[5]} {random_items[6]}")
```

ACTIVITY 4: PET PARADE

```
pet_parade_order = ['Pete the Pug', 'Sally the Siamese Cat', 'Beau the
Boxer', 'Lulu the Labrador', 'Lily the Lynx', 'Pauline the Parrot',
'Gina the Gerbil', 'Tubby the Tabby Cat']
```

Instruction 1

Go ahead and remove Gina.

Possible Solution

```
pet_parade_order.remove('Gina the Gerbil')
```

Alternative solution

```
del pet_parade_order[6]
```

Instruction 2

Move Pauline to the front of the pet parade order.

Possible Solution

```
del pet_parade_order[5]
pet_parade_order[0:0] = ['Pauline the Parrot']
```

Instruction 3

Place Mimi and Cory together so that they come after Lily.

Possible Solution

```
pet_parade_order[6:6] = ['Mimi the Maltese Cat', 'Cory the Corgi']
```

Instruction 4

Remove Lulu and Lily from the pet parade.

Possible Solution

```
del pet_parade_order[4:6]
print(f"The order of the Pet Parade is: {pet_parade_order}")
```

ANSWER KEY

Possible Solution

```
age = 10
favorite_outfit = "red dress"
favorite_hobby = "coding"
year = 2018

if year == 2018:
    print(f"It is 2018. I am currently {age} years old, love wearing
    a {favorite_outfit}, and currently, {favorite_hobby} takes up all
    my time!")
elif year == 2023:
    age += 5
    favorite_outfit = "jeans and a t-shirt"
    favorite_hobby = "making games"
    print(f"It is {year}. I am currently {age} years old, love wearing
    a {favorite_outfit}, and currently, {favorite_hobby} takes up all
    my time!")
elif year == 2028:
    age += 10
    favorite_outfit = "bike shorts and a shirt"
    favorite_hobby = "mountain biking"
    print(f"It is {year}. I am currently {age} years old, love wearing
    a {favorite_outfit}, and currently, {favorite_hobby} takes up all
    my time!")
elif year == 2033:
    age += 15
    favorite_outfit = "black dress"
    favorite_hobby = "playing the piano"
    print(f"It is {year}. I am currently {age} years old, love wearing
    a {favorite_outfit}, and currently, {favorite_hobby} takes up all
    my time!")
elif year == 2038:
    age += 20
    favorite_outfit = "white dress"
    favorite_hobby = "traveling"
    print(f"It is {year}. I am currently {age} years old, love wearing
    a {favorite_outfit}, and currently, {favorite_hobby} takes up all
    my time!")
```

ANSWER KEY

ACTIVITY 6: SLICING AND DICING

Possible Solution

```
slicing_area = []
dicing_area = []

crate_1 = ['onions', 'peppers', 'mushrooms', 'apples', 'peaches']
crate_2 = ['lemons', 'limes', 'broccoli', 'cauliflower', 'tangerines']
crate_3 = ['squash', 'potatoes', 'cherries', 'cucumbers', 'carrots']
```

Crate 1 Solution

```
slicing_area.append(crate_1[3])
slicing_area.append(crate_1[4])
dicing_area.append(crate_1[0])
dicing_area.append(crate_1[1])
dicing_area.append(crate_1[2])
```

Crate 2 Solution

```
dicing_area[3:3] = crate_2[2:4]
slicing_area[2:2] = crate_2[0:2]
slicing_area.append(crate_2[4])
```

Crate 3 Solution

```
dicing_area[5:5] = crate_3[0:2]
slicing_area.append(crate_3[2])
dicing_area[7:7] = crate_3[3:5]

print(f"Vegetables: {dicing_area}")
print(f"Fruits: {slicing_area}")
```

ACTIVITY 7: TO CHANGE OR NOT TO CHANGE
Collection 1

Possible Solution

```
person = ['Adrienne', 'Tacke', 'brown', 'black', 10, 10]
```

ANSWER KEY

```python
print(f"{person} are stored in a list!")
```

Collection 2

Possible Solution

```python
favorite_animals = ['cats', 'dogs', 'turtles', 'bunnies']
```

Collection 3

Possible Solution

```python
rainbow_colors = ('red', 'orange', 'yellow', 'green', 'blue',
'indigo', 'violet')

print(f"{rainbow_colors} are stored in a tuple!")
```

CHAPTER 4 ☆ CHALLENGES

CHALLENGE 1: CHOOSE YOUR ADVENTURE

Possible Solution

```python
name = "Adrienne"

print(f"Welcome to {name}'s Choose Your Own Adventure game! As you
follow the story, you will be presented with choices that decide your
fate. Take care and choose wisely! Let's begin.")

print("You find yourself in a dark room with 2 doors. The first door
is red, the second is white!")

door_choice = input("Which door do you want to choose? red=red door or
white=white door")

if door_choice == "red":
```

```
print("Great, you walk through the red door and are now in future!
You meet a scientist that gives you a mission of helping him save
the world!")

choice_one = input("What do you want to do? 1=Accept or 2=Decline")

if choice_one=="1":
    print("""_____SUCCESS_____
    You helped the scientist to save the world! In gratitude, the
    scientist builds a time machine and sends you home!""")
else:
    print("""_____GAME OVER_____
    Too bad! You declined the scientist's offer and now you are
    stuck in the future!""")
else:
    print("Great, you walked through the white door and now you are in
    the past! You meet a princess that asks you to go on a quest.")
    quest_choice = input("Do you want to accept her offer and go on the
    quest, or do you want to stay where you are? 1=Accept and go on
    quest or 2=Stay")

    if quest_choice=="1":
        print("The princess thanks you for accepting her offer. You
        begin the quest.")
    else:
        print("""_____GAME OVER_____
        Well, I guess your story ends here!""")
```

CHAPTER 5 ★ ACTIVITIES

ACTIVITY 1: THERE'S A LOOP FOR THAT!

Possible Solution

```
people = ['Mario', 'Peach', 'Luigi', 'Daisy', 'Toad', 'Yoshi']
desserts = ['Star Pudding', 'Peach Pie', 'Popsicles', 'Honey Cake',
'Cookies', 'Jelly Beans']
```

```
for i in range(len(people)):
    name = people[i]
    dessert = desserts[i]
    print(f"Hi! My name is {name}. My favorite dessert is {dessert}.")
```

ACTIVITY 2: LOOP DE LOOP, WHICH HULA HOOP LOOP?

Possible Solution

```
nachos_friends = ['athletic', 'not athletic', 'older', 'athletic',
'younger', 'athletic', 'not athletic', 'older', 'athletic', 'older',
'athletic']

hula_hoops_by_swings = 0
hula_hoops_by_basketball_court = 0
for i in range(len(nachos_friends)):
    if nachos_friends[i] == 'athletic' or nachos_friends[i] ==
    'younger':
        hula_hoops_by_swings += 1
    elif nachos_friends[i] == 'not athletic' or nachos_friends[i] ==
    'older':
        hula_hoops_by_basketball_court += 1

print(f"Cats at hula hoops by swings: {hula_hoops_by_swings}")
print(f"Cats at hula hoops by basketball court:
{hula_hoops_by_basketball_court}")
```

ACTIVITY 3: IFFY LEGS

Possible Solution

```
has_zero_legs = 0
has_two_legs = 0
has_four_legs = 0

animals = [4, 0, 2, 4, 2, 0, 2, 4, 4, 2, 0, 2, 4]
for i in range(len(animals)):
    if animals[i] == 0:
```

```
            has_zero_legs += 1
        elif animals[i] == 2:
            has_two_legs += 1
        elif animals[i] == 4:
            has_four_legs += 1

animal_summary = f'''
Animals with no legs: {has_zero_legs}
Animals with two legs: {has_two_legs}
Animals with four legs: {has_four_legs}
'''

print(animal_summary)
```

ACTIVITY 4: PASSWORD-PROTECTED SECRET MESSAGE

Possible Solution

```
password = 'cupcakes'
guess = ''
secret_message = 'Tomorrow, I will bring cookies for me and you at
lunch to share!'
while guess != password:
    print('What is the password?')
    guess = input()
print(f"Correct password! The secret message is: {secret_message}")
```

ACTIVITY 5: GUESS THE NUMBER GAME

Possible Solution

```
import random

number = random.randint(1, 100)
number_of_guesses = 0
```

ANSWER KEY

```
while number_of_guesses < 10:
    print('Guess a number between 1 and 100:')
    guess = input()
    guess = int(guess)
    number_of_guesses = number_of_guesses + 1

    if guess == number:
            print("Whoo! That's the magic number!")
            break
if number_of_guesses >= 10:
print(f"Aww, you ran out of guesses. The magic number was {number}.")
```

ACTIVITY 6: LOOPING LETTERS

Possible Solution

```
full_name = 'Adrienne Tacke'
number_of_a = 0
number_of_e = 0
number_of_i = 0
number_of_o = 0
number_of_u = 0

for letter in full_name:
    if letter.lower() == 'a':
            number_of_a += 1
    elif letter.lower() == 'e':
            number_of_e += 1
    elif letter.lower() == 'i':
            number_of_i += 1
    elif letter.lower() == 'o':
            number_of_o += 1
    elif letter.lower() == 'u':
            number_of_u += 1
```

ANSWER KEY

```
totals = f'''
Total number of As: {number_of_a}
Total number of Es: {number_of_e}
Total number of Is: {number_of_i}
Total number of Os: {number_of_o}
Total number of Us: {number_of_u}

'''

print(totals)
```

CHAPTER 5 ★ CHALLENGES

CHALLENGE 2: AN EVEN BETTER GUESS THE NUMBER GAME

Possible Solution

```
import random
number = random.randint(1, 100)
number_of_guesses = 0
number_of_chances = 20
while number_of_guesses < number_of_chances:
    print('Guess a number between 1 and 100:')
    guess = input()
    guess = int(guess)
    number_of_guesses = number_of_guesses + 1
    if guess < number:
        print('Your guess is too low')
    if guess > number:
        print('Your guess is too high')
```

```
    if guess == number:
        print("Whoo! That's the magic number!")
        break
    print(f"Darn, that wasn't the right number. You have {number_
    of_chances - number_of_guesses} chances left to guess the magic
    number!")
print(f"Aww, you ran out of guesses. The magic number was {number}.")
```

CHAPTER 6 ★ ACTIVITIES

ACTIVITY 2: FORTUNE-TELLER

Possible Solution

```
import turtle
import random

pointer = turtle.Turtle()
pointer.turtlesize(3, 3, 2)
pen = turtle.Turtle()
spin_amount = random.randint(1,360)
pen.penup()

pen.goto(200,0)
pen.pendown()
pen.write('Yes!', font=('Open Sans', 30))
pen.penup()

pen.goto(-400, 0)
pen.pendown()
pen.write('Absolutely Not!', font=('Open Sans', 30))
pen.penup()
```

195

```
pen.goto(-100, 300)
pen.pendown()
pen.write('Uhh, Maybe?', font=('Open Sans', 30))
pen.penup()

pen.goto(0, -200)
pen.pendown()
pen.write('Yes, but after 50 years!', font=('Open Sans', 30))
pen.ht()
pointer.right(spin_amount)
```

ACTIVITY 3: RAINBOW TURTLES!

Possible Solution

```
import turtle
turtle = turtle.Turtle()
turtle.turtlesize(2, 2, 2)
turtle.shape('turtle')
turtle.penup()

for i in range(7):
    turtle.forward(50)
    if i == 0:
        turtle.color('red')
    elif i == 1:
        turtle.color('orange')
    elif i == 2:
        turtle.color('yellow')
    elif i == 3:
        turtle.color('green')
    elif i == 4:
        turtle.color('blue')
    elif i == 5:
        turtle.color('indigo')
    elif i == 6:
        turtle.color('violet')
    turtle.stamp()
```

ANSWER KEY

Possible Solution

```
import turtle
pen = turtle.Turtle()
pen.color('purple')
pen.begin_fill()
pen.circle(100)
pen.end_fill()
pen.color('blue')
pen.begin_fill()
pen.circle(50)
pen.end_fill()
pen.color('red')
pen.begin_fill()
pen.circle(20)
pen.end_fill()
```

ACTIVITY 5: TOOGA'S HOUSE

Possible Solution

```
import turtle
tooga = turtle.Turtle()
tooga.turtlesize(2, 2, 2)
tooga.shape('turtle')
tooga.color('green')
tooga.penup()

pen = turtle.Turtle()
pen.pensize(10)
pen.color('yellow')
pen.penup()
pen.forward(100)
pen.left(90)
pen.pendown()
pen.forward(100)
pen.color('red')
pen.left(45)
```

ANSWER KEY

```
pen.forward(150)
pen.left(90)
pen.forward(150)
pen.left(45)
pen.color('yellow')
pen.forward(200)
pen.left(90)
pen.forward(210)
pen.left(90)
pen.forward(100)
```

CHAPTER 6 ★ CHALLENGES

CHALLENGE 1: TOOGA'S TRAVELS

Possible Solution

```
import turtle
import random

turtle.colormode(255)

turtle.Screen().setup(1000, 1000)
turtle.Screen().bgcolor(35, 58, 119)

divider_pen = turtle.Turtle()
divider_pen.color(255, 212, 31)
divider_pen.pensize(10)
divider_pen.back(500)
divider_pen.forward(1000)
divider_pen.ht()

pen = turtle.Turtle()
pen.penup()
pen.ht()
pen.goto(-200,300)
pen.color(255, 215, 0)
pen.pensize(5)
```

```
tooga = turtle.Turtle()
tooga.shape('turtle')
tooga.color(9, 185,13)
tooga.pencolor(0, 128, 0)
tooga.turtlesize(3, 3, 3)

tooga.penup()
tooga.goto(0, -100)

def draw_star():
    pen.pendown()
    for i in range(5):
        pen.forward(100)
        pen.right(144)
    pen.penup()
    pen.goto(pen.xcor() + 200, pen.ycor() + 20)
    return
tooga.left(90)
for i in range(1, 6):
    tooga.forward(150)
    cloudy_night = random.choice([True, False])
    print(f"is cloudy? {cloudy_night}")
    turtle.delay(30)
    if (cloudy_night != True):
        draw_star()
    tooga.right(180)
    tooga.forward(150)
    turtle.delay(50)
    tooga.right(180)
```

ANSWER KEY

CHAPTER 7 ☆ ACTIVITIES

ACTIVITY 1: SUPER FUNCTION!

Possible Solution

```
def superpower(name, power):
    print(f"Hi, I'm Super {name} and my superpower is {power}!")
superpower("Adrienne", "coding")
```

ACTIVITY 2: FUNNY FUNCTIONS

Possible Solution

```
def funny_greeting(color, dessert):
    print(f"My favorite dessert is {color} because it tastes so good
    and my favorite color is {dessert} because it is very pretty!")

funny_greeting("red", "blueberry pie")
```

ACTIVITY 3: WHAT TIME IS IT OVER THERE?

Possible Solution

```
from datetime import datetime
from datetime import timedelta

def world_times():
    my_city = datetime.now()
    berlin = my_city + timedelta(hours=9)
    baguio = my_city + timedelta(hours=15)
    tokyo = my_city + timedelta(hours=16)
    all_times = f'''It is {my_city:%I:%M} in my city.
    That means it's {berlin:%I:%M} in Berlin, {baguio:%I:%M} in Baguio
    City and {tokyo:%I:%M} in Tokyo!'''
    print(all_times)

world_times()
```

ANSWER KEY

ACTIVITY 4: FACTORIAL FUNCTION

Possible Solution

```
def factorial(number):
    result = 1
    while number >= 1:
        result = result * number
        number = number - 1
    return result
```

ACTIVITY 5: CUPCAKECOOKIE

Possible Solution

```
def dessert_sorter(desserts):
    for i in range(desserts):
        if i % 5 == 0 and i % 3 == 0:
            print("cupcakecookie")
        elif i % 3 == 0:
            print("cupcake")
        elif i % 5 == 0:
            print("cookie")
dessert_sorter(200)
```

ACTIVITY 6: DRAWING GAME BOARDS

Possible Solution

```
def print_horiz_line():
    print(" --- " * board_size)

def print_vert_line():
    print("|    " * (board_size + 1))

board_size = int(input("What size of game board?"))

for index in range(board_size):
```

```
        print_horiz_line()
        print_vert_line()

    print(" --- " * board_size)
```

ACTIVITY 7: ROCK PAPER SCISSORS

Possible Solution

```python
print("Welcome to the Rock Paper Scissors Game!")
player_1 = "Adrienne"
player_2 = "Mario"

def compare(item_1, item_2):
    if item_1 == item_2:
        return("It's a tie!")
    elif item_1 == 'rock':
        if item_2 == 'scissors':
            return("Rock wins!")
        else:
            return("Paper wins!")
    elif item_1 == 'scissors':
        if item_2 == 'paper':
            return("Scissors win!")
        else:
        return("Rock wins!")
    elif item_1 == 'paper':
        if item_2 == 'rock':
            return("Paper wins!")
        else:
            return("Scissors win!")
    else:
        return("Uh, that's not valid! You have not entered rock,
        paper or scissors.")
```

ANSWER KEY

```
player_1_choice = input("%s, rock, paper or scissors?" % player_1)
player_2_choice = input("%s, rock, paper or scissors?" % player_2)

print(compare(player_1_choice, player_2_choice))
```

CHAPTER 7 ☆ CHALLENGES

- -

CHALLENGE 1: HANGMAN GAME

Possible Solution

```
import time
name = input("What is your name?")
print(f"Hello, {name}. Time to play hangman!")
time.sleep(1)
print("Start guessing...")
time.sleep(0.5)

word = "secret"
guesses = ''
turns = 10
while turns > 0:
    failed = 0
    for char in word:
        if char in guesses:
            print(char)
        else:
            print("_")
            failed += 1
    if failed == 0:
        print("You won")
        break
    guess = input("Guess a character:")
    guesses += guess
```

```
if guess not in word:
    turns -= 1
    print("Wrong guess")
    print(f"You have {turns} more guesses remaining")
    if turns == 0:
        print("You Lose")
```

CHALLENGE 2: TURTLE RACE!

Possible Solution

```
from turtle import *
from random import randint
speed()
penup()
goto(-140, 140)

for step in range(15):
    write(step, align='center')
    right(90)
    for num in range(8):
        penup()
        forward(10)
        pendown()
        forward(10)
    penup()
    backward(160)
    left(90)
    forward(20)

ruby = Turtle()
ruby.color('red')
ruby.shape('turtle')
```

```
ruby.penup()
ruby.goto(-160, 100)
ruby.pendown()
for turn in range(10):
    ruby.right(36)

lily = Turtle()
lily.color('blue')
lily.shape('turtle')

lily.penup()
lily.goto(-160, 70)
lily.pendown()

for turn in range(72):
    lily.left(5)

tooga = Turtle()
tooga.shape('turtle')
tooga.color('green')

tooga.penup()
tooga.goto(-160, 40)
tooga.pendown()

for turn in range(60):
    tooga.right(6)

juju = Turtle()
juju.shape('turtle')
juju.color('orange')

juju.penup()
juju.goto(-160, 10)
juju.pendown()
```

```
for turn in range(30):
    juju.left(12)

for turn in range(100):
    ruby.forward(randint(1,5))
    lily.forward(randint(1,5))
    tooga.forward(randint(1,5))
    juju.forward(randint(1,5))
```

ANSWER KEY

GLOSSARY

This glossary provides the definitions for many key terms and concepts discussed in this book. Though some words may look familiar, keep in mind that their definitions here are within the context of Python programming.

additive: refers to the process of creating colors on a computer by adding different levels of light together

addition assignment operator: an operator (**+=**) used to make mutations, or changes, by adding to a variable

and operator: a logical operator that determines if both values being compared are True

arithmetic operators: a set of operators that allow you to perform mathematical equations

assignment: the action of setting a piece of information or data to a variable

bit: the smallest unit of data a computer can hold (8 bits = 1 byte)

bits: plural of bit, meaning more than one bit

Boolean type: a data type in Python that can be either True or False

Boolean expression: a condition that results in a True or False result

braces: reserved characters { } used to hold variables in formatted string literals

brackets: reserved characters [ ] used to hold a list's collection of objects or to access an index

break: used with loops, the keyword used to immediately stop repeating the loop and break out of it

bugs: mistakes or issues in code that cause it to act in an unintended way

built-in functions: prewritten , ready-to-use code made available by the Python language

byte: in computing, a unit of measurement the computer uses to represent information

call: used with functions, the action to run code at that point in time

comment: a piece of code marked with a hash character (#) that is not meant to be executed by the computer. Useful for debugging and including informational reminders about what the code is doing

comparison operators: a set of operators that help us compare one value with another

concatenation: the process of combining two things together, usually strings

debugging: the process of investigating and determining the root causes of issues in our code that cause it to act in a way we don't intend

decimal system: a number system that uses 10 different symbols to represent and create all numbers

degrees: in math, a unit of measurement based on angles within a circle

division by zero: a mathematical operation where you try to divide a number by zero; will result in a ZeroDivisionError in Python

dot notation: a way to show that certain blocks of code are related to each other

else if (elif) statement: a basic code block that allows you to check for a different Boolean expression and that is always used after an initial if statement

ending index: in the programming concept of slicing, the stopping or last index to take

equal-to operator: a comparison operator (==) that determines if the value on the left of the operator is the same as the value on the right of the operator

escape characters: special characters that alert the computer to ignore some tricky or troublesome code

execute: to run or have the computer carry out an action

exponentiation: the process of raising an integer to specified power, which uses the ** operator

extent: in the circle() function (from the Turtle module), the angle at which to draw the circle

factorial: the resulting number of an integer multiplied by all the integers below it

floating point numbers: a numeric type in Python that can have whole and fractional parts and that is written using decimal points

floats: the shorter and more common reference to floating point numbers

font: a set of type (letter, numbers, and symbols) of a common style and size

for loop: a basic code block that allows you to repeat some code a specific number of times

f-strings: short for "formatted strings." An advanced way to print strings that allows you to use variables, multiple lines, and whitespace in the resulting string

function: a reusable code block that can do something specific or return a value

greater-than operator: a comparison operator (**>**) that determines if the value on the left of the operator is larger than the value on the right of the operator

greater-than-or-equal-to operator: a comparison operator (**>=**) that determines if the value on the left of the operator is larger or the same as the value on the right of the operator

hexadecimal color: a 6-digit number that represents a color, with each pair in the 6-digit number representing a number equivalent to an RGB value

hexadecimal system: a number system that uses 16 different symbols to represent and create all numbers

I/O: the concept of input and output, where pieces of information or data are used to create or do something

IDE: an acronym for integrated development environment

IDLE: an acronym for integrated development and learning environment, which is the tool that helps you write, debug, and run Python code

if statements: a basic code block that allows you to control the path of your code by checking a Boolean expression

immutable: unable to be changed

import: special keyword used to bring other modules or functions into your code so you can use them

importing: the coding practice of making code in other files available for you to use, which uses the import keyword followed by the module being brought in

increment: the action of adding or increasing by 1

209

indentation: the coding practice of aligning related lines of code using whitespace, usually achieved by pressing the TAB key

index: a number that represents the position of an object within a list or tuple

indices: the plural form of index, meaning more than one index

infinite loop: an unwanted and unending loop that continues to repeat its code forever (can be ended by pressing CTRL + C)

in operator: a membership operator that determines if a value is part of a list or tuple and checks for positive confirmation that something exists

input: information or data we provide to the computer to process

instance: in object-oriented programming, a copy of a class

int: in Python, the shortened form of integer

integer: a basic data type in Python that represents whole numbers. Also considered a numeric type

iterating: the action of repeating or going through a collection of objects one by one

iteration: when iterating, one full cycle of repeated code

iterator: in for or while loops, the counter variable used to keep track of the number of cycles that have been repeated

less-than operator: a comparison operator (**<**) that determines if the value on the left of the operator is smaller than the value on the right of the operator

less-than-or-equal-to operator: a comparison operator (**<=**) that determines if the value on the left of the operator is smaller or the same as the value on the right of the operator

line break: a new line in code

line feed: similar to line break; a new line in code

list: a basic data type in Python that uses brackets [] to hold a collection of objects

logical operators: a set of operators used to compare True or False operands

membership operators: a set of operators used to determine if specific content is or is not in the input

module: a group or collection of reusable code, usually related and made up of functions

modulus: an arithmetic operator that performs a division operation and returns the remainder from that operation

mutable: able to be changed

mutation: in programming, a change or modification

not-equal-to operator: a comparison operator (**!=**) that determines if the value on the left of the operator is not the same to the value on the right of the operator

not in operator: a membership operator that determines if a value is not part of a list or tuple and checks for positive confirmation that something does not exist

not operator: a logical operator that determines if the value being compared is False

numeric types: one of the basic data types in the Python language that is used to represent numbers

object-oriented programming: a programming style in which code is organized into groups like building blocks

operands: values that have actions performed on them

operators: special symbols or keywords that represent an action

order of operations: based on the rules of precedence in math, this is the set of rules the computer follows to determine which calculations to perform first in a long line of math equations

or operator: a logical operator that determines if at least one of two values being compared is True

output: the resulting words, numbers, or actions that a computer gives back after we ask it to do something

parameter: used in a function, this is a piece of a data passed in as input that the function will do something with

power: in math, the number of times to multiply a number to a certain exponent

primary additive colors: in computing, these are red, green, and blue

radius: in the circle() function, the size of the circle you want to draw

register: a place within the computer's central processing unit (CPU) where it can hold information

remainder: in math and while using division, this value is the remaining amount that is left over in a division equation that is not evenly divided

return value: the output or resulting data a function gives back after being called

reusability: the concept of being able to use code over and over again without much issue

RGB color model: one of the color models used to select colors in computer coding

rules of precedence: based in mathematics, the order of importance of certain mathematical operations

semicircle: a half circle equal to 180 degrees

shell: the interactive window that allows you to write Python code within it and then see the results of your code right away

single quotes: special characters used to surround strings (')

slice range: the specific range of items to take when slicing

slicing: the action of taking a specific range of items within a list or tuple

starting index: in the programming concept of slicing, the starting or first index to take

step: in the circle() function, the number of units to skip

str: the abbreviated version of the string data type

string: a basic data type in Python that is used to represent characters or what we know as text

syntax error: a mistake in code that the computer cannot understand

triple quotes: special characters used with strings to allow multi-line strings (''') or (""")

tuple: an unchangeable data type that can hold a collection of objects and uses parentheses ( ) to hold its objects

type: a designation or label that helps the computer understand what kind of input we are giving it

type error: a mistake in the code that is related to an incorrect or unexpected data type

variable: an object that allows us to keep track of information

while loop: another type of loop that keeps repeating a specific block of code as long as a Boolean expression continues to be true

zero division error: a mistake in the code that occurs when you try to divide by 0

RESOURCES

MATH MODULE

This is a built-in module that comes with the Python language. Much like the **turtle** module, the **math module** provides functions that are ready for us to use and are commonly used in Python programming. As its name implies, this module provides many math functions, including **sum()**, **sqrt()**, and **pow()**.

The **sum()** function accepts a list of integers as a parameter and returns the total of all the integers in the list. It's a ready-made function for adding.

The **sqrt(x)** function accepts an integer and returns its square root. For example, using **sqrt(81)** would return a value of 9.

The **pow(x, y)** function is another useful function that accepts two parameters and uses the exponentiation operator to return the x parameter to the y power. For example, using **pow(3, 4)** would return a value of 81. It does the same thing as multiplying 3 x 3 x 3 x 3.

These functions are the most used ones in the math module, but there are many more. Go to Mathematical Functions in the Python Standard Library (https://docs .python.org/3/library/math.html) to see the full list!

RANDOM MODULE

Another built-in module that comes in handy for games and programs is the **random module**. As you can guess, it provides functions that help with the generation of random data. For our purposes, you can focus on the **randint()** functions from this module. Yes, "randint" stands for random integer!

randint(x, y): This function accepts two parameters: a starting number and an ending number. When you use this function, it picks a random number for you to use between the starting number and up to (but not including) the ending number. We used this function in our Guess the Number Game (page 108) to ask the computer to pick a random number for us to guess!

DATETIME MODULE

Another very useful module that is readily available in the Python language is called the **datetime module**. This module gives us many different functions to use that deal with time, dates, and changes to time and dates. In this book, we've used a few common datetime functions, including the **now()** function and the **timedelta()** function.

The **now** function returns the current date and time.

The **timedelta** function allows us to manipulate time according to a specific unit we set. We used this function in our What Time Is It Over There? activity (page 200).

Just like the math module, the datetime module offers so many other useful functions that can be helpful in your programs. Be sure to check out the Basic Date and Time Types in the Python Standard Library (https://docs.python.org/3/library/datetime.html) to see the full list. (Don't worry if the documentation sounds a little scary. As long as you can find the name of the function and what parameters it accepts, you should be able to figure out what it does. You can even experiment with the different functions to see what they do.)

WEBSITES

Here is a variety of websites to visit to further boost your programming and Python knowledge!

PYTHON RESOURCES

There are many resources available that you can use to test your Python knowledge even beyond this book. Here's a list of them and more information about what you can find in each one:

- Practice Python (PracticePython.org): This great website has many practice problems and projects that you can tackle using Python.

- Code.org (Code.org/learn): This resource offers fun games and activities to try on your own with Python.

- Real Python (RealPython.com): This website has many articles that focus on different programming principles in Python. It's a great complement to the information in this book.

- Python Documentation (Docs.Python.org/3/contents.html): This is the official documentation for the Python 3 language. It may be a bit advanced, but it is the official source and is good to know about.

CODING RESOURCES

For more general resources that teach coding, check out these sites:

- Code.org Course Catalog (Studio.Code.org/courses): This site has so many excellent coding resources for beginners. Choose your age range or skill level, and there will be plenty of content for you to enjoy!

- Scratch (Scratch.MIT.edu): Scratch is a project by the Lifelong Kindergarten Group at the MIT Media Lab. It is a visual programming language that can help you learn programming concepts in a different way.

- Code Academy (CodeCademy.com): This site is an interactive tool that helps you learn how to code in other languages. Get real-time feedback as you solve coding puzzles and learn how to write another language's code.

RESOURCES

INDEX

INDEX

INDEX

ACKNOWLEDGMENTS

Mario: *mahal,* thank you for staying up with me all those nights. Even though you felt just as tired after work and your eyes grew heavier the longer you stayed up, you kept me company, brought me coffee and cake, and helped me pull through and finish this book. Thank you so much. I love you!

Jillie: You were the inspiration and motivation for this book. Every time I felt too tired to finish a section or review an activity, I remembered how excited you were at the prospect of learning how to code from a book by your sister! It kept me on track and helped me make sure I wrote a book that was good enough for you. I love you!

Lucie: I am so happy you are with Jillie and are helping her navigate this part of her life. I am also so proud of the big sister you have become to her. Thank you for filling in for me as the "eldest" sister for all these years. I can't wait until you both are closer to me! I love you!

Mom: For always being there and for supporting me through every part of my life. I love you!

Tito Joel: For always supporting me and for being as excited about this book as I am!

Tito JP: For never hesitating to let me crash at your place and for supporting my tech career!

Tito Gerry: For inspiring me to be ambitious and always reach for the stars!

Ma Angie: For everything you do and more. I hope this book makes you proud. I love you, Dona Angie!

To all of my Instagram followers: Thank you for your continued support. Without you, this opportunity wouldn't even be possible and this book wouldn't exist!

Susan Randol: From initial milestone feedback to your flexibility with deadlines, I appreciate everything you have done to help make this book a success. Your enthusiasm for the book made it a joy to work with you. Thank you, and I hope to work on a JavaScript book with you in the future!

Patty Consolazio: You are quite the trooper for going through my first book and pointing out all of the inconsistencies, missing bits of information, and parts that were not quite clear. This is greatly appreciated, as I not only want to educate readers but inspire and excite them about the power of code. Without your help, that would not be possible. Thank you!

Merideth Harte: Your patience and flexibility were incredibly nice to work with, especially since my book was reliant on accurate screenshots! Thank you for your quick work and quick thinking!

Amir Abou Roumié: Your illustrations brought my book to life! Thank you for creating such wonderful artwork; I'm honored to have your work in my book!

Vanessa Putt: Our initial conversations and further discussions about this book were always pleasant. Your responses were quick, and you answered all of my questions in full detail. You even discussed my idea for a JavaScript book, which has some possibility of being created, and that is so awesome! Thank you for everything!

Marthine Satris: Thank you for taking a chance and sending me that email for a possible chat about a book. I'm certainly glad you sent that email!

ABOUT THE AUTHOR

Software engineer, writer, and STEM education advocate **ADRIENNE B. TACKE** is a Filipina technologist who has been professionally developing software for over eight years. As a Code.org volunteer in Las Vegas, she regularly speaks to students of all ages about the power of code and specifically encourages young women and girls to explore a career in software engineering. She is also a contributing writer for online tech publications such as HackerNoon and CodeBurst. *Coding for Kids: Python* is her first book (but certainly not her last!).